MAKING BLACK SCIENTISTS

Making Black Scientists

A CALL TO ACTION

Marybeth Gasman

Thai-Huy Nguyen

Harvard University Press

CAMBRIDGE, MASSACHUSETTS

LONDON, ENGLAND

2019

During our visits to the various Black college campuses in this book,
we heard a common phrase from faculty members who worked closely
with African American students pursuing degrees in science:
"We make Black scientists here."
Our book's title stems from this phrase.

First printing

Library of Congress Cataloging-in-Publication Data

Names: Gasman, Marybeth, author. | Nguyen, Thai-Huy, 1983- author.
Title: Making black scientists : a call to action / Marybeth Gasman,
Thai-Huy Nguyen.
Description: Cambridge, Massachusetts : Harvard University Press, 2019. |
Includes bibliographical references and index.
Identifiers: LCCN 2019002607 | ISBN 9780674916586 (alk. paper)
Subjects: LCSH: Minorities in science—United States. | Minorities—Education
(Higher)—United States. | Science—Study and teaching
(Higher)—United States. | College students, Black—United States. |
African American universities and colleges.
Classification: LCC Q149.U5 G37 2019 | DDC 507.1/173—dc23
LC record available at https://lccn.loc.gov/2019002607

CONTENTS

MAKING BLACK SCIENTISTS

Introduction

Race, Racism, and American Higher Education

JESSE, WHO LOVED SCIENCE AND MATH from an early age, enrolled at a public research university in California to study engineering as an undergraduate student. She hoped to pursue a career in science and believed that she had the necessary skills and the drive to be successful. Jesse was excited about her classes, although she noticed that most of the professors and students did not look like her. Jesse is African American.[1] Most of the students in her classes were White; some were Asian American. Having grown up in the heart of Los Angeles, Jesse had attended a diverse high school, so she was accustomed to being around students from a variety of racial and ethnic backgrounds. She had very few African American teachers or teachers of color prior to college, so she was not surprised that most of her engineering teachers were White and men. Despite occasional racist comments from peers and teachers, which her parents had prepared her for from a young age, Jesse was always a high-performing student, studying each day and night to do her best in her classes. She was confident in her ability to perform alongside other students.

Jesse's college professors were traditional in their approach to teaching, often relying on lecturing and PowerPoint slides. Jesse learned early on the enormity of content that she alone was responsible for absorbing, understanding, and mastering. In response, she was inclined to form study groups, studying with classmates for the purpose of effective learning and support. In theory, this might seem like a good idea, but for Jesse it led to pain. When she approached her classmates in several different courses, not a single student accepted the invitation to study with her. She found that puzzling. And when she asked why, one of her classmates responded, "I don't want to work with a Black person because it will bring my grade down." Jesse was devastated by the comment, knowing that her classmates were the individuals that she would work with in the future as an engineer. They sent her a message that she did not belong in engineering or at the university.

From Jesse's perspective, not only did her classmates hold racist views about her, but she believed that they did not realize how their success was intertwined with her success. Jesse wondered why they did not understand that she might bring fresh and innovative ideas to their study sessions and that her skills might strengthen their performance rather than bring them down. Perhaps Jesse's classmates were blinded by American society's racist images of African Americans—images that often fail to portray students like Jesse as having value, as intelligent, and as beneficial to their learning environment. Perhaps Jesse's classmates were, in part, also hindered by a culture of STEM (science, technology, engineering, and mathematics), steeped in personal and independent achievement, that was reinforced by faculty members and staff. In such a culture it can be difficult to embrace the idea of working with others, especially with others who seem very different from themselves, and especially when institutions privilege individual achievement.[2]

Eventually Jesse became overwhelmed by how her classmates were treating her. She turned to faculty members for support, but they suggested working with different students, not realizing that the problem was systemic. Jesse was the only Black woman in a sea of students who apparently did not want anything to do with her. Waiting in a long line to meet with her professors during office hours also made it less likely for her to see them as an accessible source of support. She finished her degree, but instead of following her dream of working as an engineer, Jesse decided to pursue a graduate degree in education, studying the experiences of African American women in STEM majors, specifically the conditions that limit and foster their success. Although Jesse took a different pathway, one that gave her the opportunity to address system-level barriers to achievement and to work toward a more inclusive culture of STEM, her experience highlights the broader issue of racial inequality and unequal opportunity in college and in the STEM fields.[3]

The racist treatment Jesse endured in college can be traced back to America's history of enslaving, degrading, and dehumanizing Black bodies and minds.[4] It has been more than a century since the abolishment of slavery and slightly more than half a century since racial segregation was deemed unconstitutional by the U.S. Supreme Court in *Brown v. Board of Education*. Many saw Barack Obama's presidency as a significant victory against racial inequality, but skin color continues to determine the opportunities and challenges people face in pursuing the lives they desire. As Jesse and so many other Black Americans know, being Black in America means living in a society that regularly questions your motives and intelligence—despite your experiences and credentials—because of the color of your skin. It means having the police called on you for barbecuing in the park or being stopped in a store or on the highway because the way you "look" confirms the dominant, racist narratives that some hold about Black communities as breeding grounds for criminals. It means having limited access to quality healthcare or being relegated to inadequately resourced schools that offer little means for upward social mobility. Being Black means that society will often think the worst about you and that you are to blame for your fate, given that racist narratives fail to acknowledge how systemic racism oppresses Black communities. Being Black in America means that the social and economic systems in our society will rarely benefit you or the generations that will come after you, because they were not built to do so. In fact, schools, colleges, and universities often uphold these systems of inequality.[5]

Despite their best, public intentions to increase access and success for students from all racial backgrounds, colleges and universities, which are significant engines of upward social mobility, often reproduce racial inequality and further inequity.[6] Through the assumptions and expectations that shape the criteria for admission, the curriculum and its delivery, the obsession with college rankings, and the cultures of White- and male-dominated fields of study, colleges and universities often fail Black students because they refuse to consider that their practices could be discriminatory at their core.[7] Until this changes, and as long as higher education is the main gateway to opportunities that can uplift individuals from their current circumstances, the underrepresentation of Blacks in the STEM workforce and the academy will endure. The battle for improved representation and achievement in STEM by Black students is rooted in a much larger racial-historical context across our nation's colleges and universities.

The Beginnings of Black Education in the United States

To understand how racism manifests in higher education, we need to consider that most of our nation's colleges and universities were not created to educate the diverse group of students currently knocking at their doors. Instead, they were designed to educate wealthy, White men.[8] The way our colleges are organized, the way we teach, those we choose to teach, and the ways we privilege certain kinds of learning, writing, and forms of knowledge are based on the origins of our colleges and universities—origins that are rooted in American racism in its earliest forms.

At the end of the Civil War in 1865, there were masses of Blacks whom the horrors of slavery had starved of any kind of formal education, yet they were hungry for learning. President Abraham Lincoln offered a plan of Reconstruction as the Civil War ended, but southern states were slow to respond and midwestern states enacted Black codes to slow migration into their areas. Although free of slavery, African Americans were deemed second-class citizens by law and actions.[9]

In March 1865, Congress established the Bureau of Refugees, Freedmen, and Abandoned Lands—the Freedmen's Bureau—which helped establish some of the nation's earliest historically Black colleges and universities (HBCUs), along with White missionary organizations from the North that sought to "civilize" Blacks and introduce them to White society.[10] Black missionary groups from churches such as the African Methodist Episcopal Church were also involved in the establishment of colleges throughout the South. Through the work of these various missionary groups and federal involvement, HBCUs were created and began to educate Blacks, providing primary, secondary, and college curricula across the South, and building a foundation for the Black middle class as we currently know it.[11] It is important to keep in mind that HBCUs were not established in ways that mirrored the predominantly White neighboring colleges and universities. Many were in church basements and one-room schoolhouses, as there was little funding allotted to the education of Blacks. Nonetheless, African American leaders and missionaries worked together to provide an education to whomever desired it.

In 1890 Congress approved the second Morrill Act, which provided funds to states to expand their higher education efforts. However, Congress stipulated that Blacks must be educated in addition to Whites in order for states to receive funding. With this stipulation, the southern states established a separate system of public Black colleges rather than integrate the preexisting predominantly White institutions (PWIs). However, the schools in these separate state systems were not equal, and most consisted of makeshift classrooms with a few teachers and no libraries—most state education funds were directed toward the PWIs. Even up to the current day, public HBCUs across all southern states have had to fight for equal state funding and equity. Some public HBCUs are still forced to educate their students with half the funding of their PWI counterparts in the same state.[12] People are often surprised by this kind of blatant racism in the twenty-first century; however, there is ample evidence to demonstrate the way systemic racism manifests and ample opportunity for states to change their funding formulas to foster increased equity.[13] Unfortunately, these changes rarely take place without court interference as states often do not place a high value on Black lives.[14]

With the ruling in *Brown v. Board of Education* in 1954, HBCUs found themselves in a precarious situation. Many of their funders—White, northern, industrial philanthropists at that point—questioned the need for HBCUs after *Brown,* assuming that integration of PWIs would soon follow the historic Supreme Court decision. Of course, integration did not come until the late 1960s and early 1970s, and even those efforts were not always welcomed. *Brown* called into question the value of HBCUs because they were seen as segregated institutions and unnecessary after the fall of legalized segregation.[15] Unfortunately, many Whites, even those with good intentions, assumed that anything Black would disappear and fold into the White world around it—that societal standards were, by default, White standards. They did not recognize the value of Black communities, their culture and history in shaping approaches to education, and what could be learned from them. Take, for instance, the discipline of sociology (especially urban sociology) in America, which has largely promoted "the fact" that its founder was the University of Chicago—despite histories demonstrating the initial and extensive influence of the Atlanta Sociological Laboratory at Atlanta University, an HBCU (now Clark Atlanta University), under the leadership of W. E. B. Du Bois, who published the first urban sociological study, *The Philadelphia Negro,* in 1889.[16] We continue to see this arrogance of intellect today in the way knowledge at and from HBCUs is often ignored as PWIs attempt to educate Black students.[17]

Many African Americans eventually chose to attend PWIs after their long-fought battles to desegregate them. Although these choices moved our nation toward integration, they also changed the perception of HBCUs for many in the country. For decades HBCUs had been lauded for their ability to produce successful Black students as they were the only place that Blacks could attend (with a few exceptions in the

Northeast).[18] With the fall of segregation, HBCUs lost many students, which led people to assume that HBCUs were not contributing in ways that they had in the past. Many, including some Blacks, began questioning the relevance of HBCUs and continue to do so.[19] And this questioning—continually reinforced by popular media and scholarship[20]—leads to a resistance to learning from HBCUs even when many of these institutions, such as Morehouse College and Xavier University in Louisiana, have a legacy of successfully educating African American students and preparing them for graduate and professional school, most prominently in the STEM fields.[21] These narratives of achievement are often lost to a system of higher education whose standards continue to privilege and reward PWIs. In this book, we ask readers to see HBCUs as incubators of talent that we can learn from if we are truly interested in promoting the achievement of African American students in the STEM fields.

Racism and Higher Education

In recent years, more Black students at PWIs are rising up and pushing back against campus climates that are not designed for them and some-times work to squash their voices, rights, and dreams. Yes, most Black students attend PWIs, and yes, many PWIs are integrated, and yet prac-tices that weed out Black students persist.[22] Most four-year PWIs have small numbers of Black students—percentages below the percentage of Blacks in the U.S. population. Few four-year PWIs have a student body that is at least 13 percent Black, yet HBCUs are accused of being segregated institutions in the twenty-first century despite having stu-dent bodies that are 13 percent White, 2 percent Latino, and 2 percent Asian American.[23] How many PWIs have interrogated their programs and policies that often hold back Black students and other racial and ethnic minorities? Very few, and many are under pressure to maintain their current campus cultures by resistant faculty, influential alumni, and wealthy donors.[24] How many PWIs have experienced or implicitly allowed racial violence against Black students in recent years? While countless racial issues were rearing their ugly heads across the nation and the Black Lives Matter movement was trying to ensure that people were "woke" around the large-scale violence, oppression, and racism against Blacks, in 2014 the online news site *Inside Higher Education* asked presidents and provosts across the nation if racism was an issue on their campuses. Ninety percent reported that "race relations were excellent or good."[25] Campus leaders are not acknowledging the forces threatening Black students' belongingness and ability to take advantage of opportunities to learn and thrive on campus.[26] Black students' success is hindered as they continue to witness and experience racial violence—frequent murders of Black people; the highly disproportionate incarceration of Black men, a system considered the "new racial caste"[27] or the election of Donald Trump, seen as giving permission to physically and verbally assault racial and religious minorities—on their college campuses. Unbeknownst to many, college is not a time where students are wholly detached from reality and personal obligation, free to pursue their passions without challenge. This is a dangerous myth. Black students and other underrepresented racial and ethnic groups are often afraid for their lives, knowing that the structural and symbolic violence against their communities can also exist in their classrooms, in residence halls, and in interactions with faculty members and other students.

Many PWIs fail Black students in major ways. Their curricula are White-centered—promoting the perspectives and histories of White scholars across the foundation of general education, relegating non-White perspectives and historic discoveries to supplemental readings or not including them at all, and neither acknowledging nor discussing race and racism. The physical and biological sciences are often portrayed as race-neutral, when, in fact, histories demonstrate how "science" was used to justify slavery and promote theories of racial inferiority.[28] If you are White, this approach can be empowering, because this White-centric form of curriculum is generally what you are accustomed to and what has nurtured and affirmed you throughout most of your education. However, if you are Black, you often feel ostracized, pushed to the margins as if your voice does not matter.[29] According to Black students who experience it daily, the lack of racially diverse curricula has a profound negative impact on their perception of their belongingness, and ultimately on their ability to learn and persist.[30] One of the reasons the curriculum at most PWIs is White-centered and delivered in ways that can alienate Black students and other racial and ethnic minorities is that 76 percent of the faculty at PWIs are White.[31]

We see the country's demographics shifting—with more Latino, Asian American, and Black students making their way to campuses—but we see very little increase in faculty diversity.[32] The lack of movement is largely the fault of one group—our current faculty members. At most colleges and universities, the faculty members are responsible for recruiting new faculty members, and generally they recruit candidates with backgrounds similar to their own in terms of education, mentors, and teaching styles, which has resulted in a largely White faculty even as the pipelines to the professoriate have become more diverse.[33] During the recruiting process, faculty often hold Black job candidates (and other racial and ethnic minorities) to higher standards, questioning where they earned their undergraduate degrees, the quality of their PhD programs (even highly selective programs), and the stature of their mentors.[34] Even faculty members who on the surface appear committed to diversity, equity, and inclusion put up roadblocks to hiring underrepresented racial and ethnic candidates by bringing up issues of quality—concerns that are rarely raised for White candidates.[35] If mentored by the "right" people and holding a degree from the "right" institution, White candidates are given the benefit of the doubt on issues—teaching, research, or publications—related to their qualifications.[36] White faculty members' regular responses of doubt to minority candidates reflect not only their biases, but an educational system that allows such behavior to occur. Some researchers suggest that implicit biases are at the core of this kind of racism, whereas others claim that it is intentional and central to Whites' upholding systems that maintain their status while oppressing others.[37]

Faculty members who know that there is systemic racism in faculty hiring processes and even whisper their support to Black colleagues, yet remain silent in public so as not to risk their own privileges in the college and university setting, can often be the most concerning.[38] Maintaining the status quo among faculty members does not help anyone, especially not students. Doing so openly reinforces the systemic racism on which our colleges and universities were built, hindering the efforts for greater inclusion on our campuses.

As PWIs see more campus unrest and growing numbers of Black students feeling ignored, our nation's HBCUs have started to see increases in enrollment. Black families, now a generation or two away from attending HBCUs, are deciding to give them another look due to what Walter Kimbrough, president of Dillard University, coins the "Missouri effect."[39] In late 2015, after years of student unrest at the University of Missouri, much of it resulting from several hate crimes against Black students, student group #ConcernedStudent1950 protested against the racially oppressive campus climate and demanded changes to the university, including a more racially inclusive curriculum, increased recruitment of Black faculty members and staff, and the resignation of the university system's president. Joined by other student groups, #ConcernedStudent1950 created a national movement that took many colleges and universities by storm. In protesting a higher education system that offered conflicting promises of an improved racial climate, students revealed the many ways they felt hurt, unacknowledged, and unwelcome. Realizing that their children are more likely to learn in environments free from a culture steeped in Whiteness and in which they are embraced and championed, more Black parents are encouraging their children to apply to HBCUs, with many ultimately choosing to attend. Parents and students also realize that HBCUs offer other important elements for learning, such as an environment expressly built for Blacks, including both a diverse curriculum and faculty—56.3 percent Black and 43.7 percent other racial and ethnic minorities and Whites—that can relate to and speak on the issues African Americans face in the United States.

Changing the Culture of STEM

When we learned of Jesse's story, we immediately began to wonder how many other African American students have had her experience of exclusion. Unfortunately, throughout this study, we found that Jesse's story, detailing her pain as the result of a racist and exclusionary culture of STEM, is all too common among African American students at PWIs.[40] The culture of STEM at many PWIs is made up of practices and forms of pedagogy that discourage minority and low-income students, diminish their sense of belonging and their capacity to persist, and ultimately limit their learning. For these students, their achievement in STEM becomes a function of how well they expend *additional* energy and focus to make sense of and navigate this culture, extra steps that are not often necessary for White, middle- to upper-class students. This very difference in experience helps explain why racial disparities in education and the underrepresentation of Blacks in the STEM workforce endure. Jesse's story of feeling that her peers doubted her intelligence, and not finding support from her professors, is common and supported by a rich canon of research.[41] We wondered: How would the STEM fields overall be different if students like Jesse were valued and affirmed rather than ignored and dismissed? Our aim in this book is to contemplate environments that value and affirm Black students. Drawing upon campus visits and interviews at ten HBCUs (Dillard University, Xavier University of Louisiana, Prairie View A&M University, North Carolina Central University, Delaware State University, Morgan State University, Claflin University, Lincoln University, Cheyney University, and Huston-Tillotson University), we offer an agenda for how a culture of STEM can look, feel, and operate in a drastically different way from more mainstream institutions and, in fact, encourage African American students to persevere and achieve, instead of isolate and dismiss them.[42] We organize this book around the very dimensions that make up this culture and argue that faculty, departments, and institutions can find critical insight and inspiration from the inner workings of these historically Black institutions. However, to be clear: these dimensions do not operate solo but work in tandem to create a holistic learning environment. Some ideas overlap because the culture of STEM at these HBCUs is interconnected and porous—a characteristic that we think can put these HBCUs in a better position to address Black students' relationship with their institutions, thereby advancing their efforts to improve the achievement of Black students in STEM. At these HBCUs, it is not that the STEM culture is less rigorous but that it *privileges* different values that drive work with students. This STEM culture at these HBCUs is by no means hidden or secret, but it is a culture that many schools do not value in the training of future scientists and leaders in STEM. We hope that this book convinces readers of its value.

Our campus visits to each of the HBCUs offered us unique opportunities to understand and make sense of the qualitative conditions that help Black students engage, learn, and thrive in STEM. Chapter 1 provides a brief background on the research related to Black students and their pursuit of STEM degrees. This background helps contextualize and undergird the importance of our findings. Chapter 2 captures the dominant belief of these HBCUs that they themselves are responsible for helping students to realize their fullest potential, no matter students' background or academic preparedness. This chapter also showcases how these institutions question the dominant assumptions that so often limit the opportunities of Black students. From there we move onto how the different assumptions that these HBCUs make about their students help drive the overall student experience in STEM. In Chapter 3 we showcase how students are encouraged to work with each other, creating a system of improved learning, accountability, and self-confidence that is framed by communal, rather than individual, achievement. We carry this idea of communal success to Chapter 4, where the dominant narrative of student success in STEM, defined by the idea and practice of exclusion, is replaced by one of deep inclusion that helps push against students' self-doubts of their capacity to persevere. Messages, however, are not without action. In Chapter 5, we report faculty members' reflections on how their teaching, advising, and support of students, and even their interactions with each other within and across departments, is first and foremost driven by a shared commitment to students. Chapter 6 looks more closely at the importance of faculty and student relationships, more specifically the importance for students to have faculty that they can relate to, both by racial and gender identity. We also extend this discussion to include ways in which non-Black faculty can address alienation with students that arise from differences in background. We then round out the core of the book with Chapter 7, which demonstrates the extended manner in which these HBCUs support the achievement of their students. Faculty see their students as fictive kin, supporting students and caring for their well-being both inside and outside the classroom as if they are their own family members. This "family" bond is also bidirectional in that students are often driven to do their best by knowing that their faculty, or "parents," are giving it their all to help them reach their goals. We then move toward a call for action with Chapter 8, which marries our critiques of higher education in this introduction with recommendations that any institutions can consider when shaping their own strategies for improving Black student achievement in STEM. The Appendix highlights the HBCUs in the study and explains the process of our work, shedding light on how we came to select the institutions and collect and analyze our data.

Our book is organized around themes related to what it takes to promote success for African American students in the STEM fields. We draw upon these institutions' practices to demonstrate an alternative narrative about Black achievement in STEM with the hope of inspiring other institutions—their faculty and staff—to critique the ways in which their everyday traditions and norms in teaching and research might unfairly penalize Black students and other students of color. Readers could be students, parents and guardians, high school teachers and counselors, professors, researchers, funders, or those merely curious about the types of strategies or a different culture of STEM that privilege the achievement of all students in the STEM fields, especially those not traditionally represented. For high school and college students who are contemplating pursuing a degree in a STEM field, we ask that you pay special attention to how students perceive and treat each other and the messages of inclusive excellence that shape how faculty members perform inside and outside the classroom. For parents and guardians, or those entrusted to advise and guide a student to and through college, we ask that you consider the quality of experience you wish for your student—acceptance and collaboration? Or possible discrimination and cut-throat competitiveness? For teachers, counselors, and professors, we ask that you consider the values of your colleagues working at HBCUs—values that shape the quality of their commitment to Black student achievement in STEM. If you feel dissonance, what might this reveal about your assumptions, your department, and your institution? For researchers and funders, we ask that as you read this book, you consider why—despite national data demonstrating the effectiveness of HBCUs in graduating Black students in STEM—PWIs are always taken as the standard by which other institutions are compared.

Although others have written about success models and practices in STEM—including famed University of Texas mathematics professor Uri Treisman, and Freeman Hrabowski, the president of the University of Maryland, Baltimore County—we are concerned that the success models and strategies are not being used at most colleges and universities.[43] This lack of use leads us to believe that many colleges and universities know the ways to ensure that African American students succeed in STEM but do not have the will to use them. If there were more will, there would be more success across the board for African American students in STEM. Given what we learned about African American success in STEM and the strategies that we present herein, we believe that institutions that are not open to changing, adopting many of these strategies, and committing to providing African American students with equity of opportunity, are not remaining true to their missions and are reinforcing systemic racism.

Racism in our society, and on our campuses, is hurting our students, but especially our Black students as they continue to suffer from our nation's original sin—slavery—and the racism that has spilled over since the vile practice was in full swing in our country. Racism on our campuses is making us fall behind as a nation, because we are no longer leaders in the world, especially in the areas of STEM. Instead of drawing upon the largest pool of students to help us create and innovate, we are providing opportunities to only a small group of students—mainly Whites and mostly men. We are forgetting that "a mind is a terrible thing to waste," as the United Negro College Fund has reminded us for years. We are withholding opportunities from young Blacks interested in the STEM fields—opportunities that could result in innovation, progress, and the growth of their communities and of our nation.[44]

Each time we fail to encourage Black students to pursue STEM degrees and refuse to believe in their potential, we are holding their communities and the nation behind. Each time faculty members refuse to teach in inclusive, innovative, collaborative, and supportive ways, we are leaving students, who require an environment that champions them, behind. Each time we neglect to reach out to colleges and universities that have a demonstrated track record for educating and graduating successful Black students to ask them how they manage this success, we do a disservice to Black students.

Overcoming American racism is challenging, and dismantling systemic racism in our colleges and universities will take a great deal of work from all corners of the academy, but finding innovative and productive ways to provide nurturing learning environments that empower Black students is not difficult. We just need to have the will and to make the choice to tap into the institutions and examples that already exist. These examples are housed at many of the nation's Black colleges and have been fostering success in STEM for decades. Many HBCUs provide a rich learning environment for all of us interested in increasing Black student achievement in STEM. They can teach us how to create STEM degree programs that build on students' interest in and desire to perform in STEM and that foster collaborative learning, drawing on the identities and backgrounds of students, and promote their success regardless of their preparation. If we are not willing to learn from successful HBCUs and admit that they have much to teach us in STEM education and overall, we are perpetuating the racist idea that PWIs are the only institutions that hold and produce knowledge and are of any value to society. Although the overall environment of these HBCUs cannot be reproduced, in this book we describe the various strategies—many very simple and straightforward—that can be adopted and adapted at colleges and universities that are committed to STEM success for Black students. We provide an agenda for success for parents, students, faculty, leaders, foundations, and communities interested in enhancing representation and performance in STEM. We focus on ensuring that Black students have the very best learning environments for excelling in the STEM fields. However, all the strategies described in this book can be used with any students and should be.

I

The State of STEM in the United States

When time is dedicated to engaging with students to understand the relationship between their lives and their potential for success in college, institutions can begin to alter the pathway for students from disadvantaged backgrounds.

—HBCU faculty member

SCIENCE, TECHNOLOGY, ENGINEERING, AND MATH, as fields of study or occupation, are markers of racial inequality. For the past decade the U.S. government has pressed its agencies—including the National Academy of Science, the National Science Foundation, and the National Institutes of Health—and prominent nonprofit organizations to identify and implement strategies to increase the number of qualified individuals to meet the demands of the workforce, including a large emphasis on the growing racial and ethnic minority populations.[1] There is little disagreement that our society, nation, and world are continually being shaped by the growing presence of technology and advances in science and healthcare. And with this growing presence comes the increase of new opportunities and the demand for sufficient

THE STATE OF STEM IN THE UNITED STATES

human capital. The push to increase STEM-educated individuals raises a series of questions about racial inequality and opportunity. Who will be able to benefit from these opportunities? What type of background will these individuals possess? Does race matter in the STEM fields?

We know that African Americans are underrepresented in the attainment of STEM degrees. Between 2004 and 2014, the number of African Americans and Blacks who received STEM degrees remained quite stagnant, constituting about 9 percent of all bachelor's degrees awarded across all STEM fields, but only 7 percent of degrees awarded in biological sciences, 6 percent in physical sciences, 5 percent awarded in mathematics and statistics, and 4 percent in engineering—whereas African Americans make up 13.2 percent of the U.S. populace.[2] What is impeding the progress of African Americans at colleges and universities? Are Black students having experiences similar to those of Jesse in her engineering program? We do not answer these questions, but we do look to HBCUs for solutions that might improve interest and success in STEM degree attainment for African American students.

HBCUs make up only 3 percent of all postsecondary institutions, and yet the 105 HBCUs contribute 17 percent of all baccalaureate degrees awarded to Black students.[3] Nearly 18 percent of Black students receiving bachelor degrees in the STEM fields are HBCU graduates. Of the degrees awarded to Black students, HBCUs award 27 percent of degrees in the biological sciences, nearly 30 percent of degrees in mathematics, 32 percent of degrees in physical sciences, and 19 percent of degrees in engineering.[4] What are HBCUs doing that most colleges and universities are not? What unique strategies do they employ in terms of the curricula and their work with students? And what can we learn from them that can help African Americans at all colleges and universities?

Neighborhood, Home, and Pre-College Contexts

We begin our discussion with the pre-college context because students do not come to college as blank slates; societal forces begin to shape their lives at birth. As mentioned in the Introduction, the disadvantages that shape the unfavorable position of Black communities in society can be traced back to the historical legacy of racial injustice that continues to penetrate the daily lives of all Americans. Blacks, as well as other underrepresented racial minorities, continue to encounter structural barriers—such as poverty, unemployment, and residential segregation—that inextricably constrain their opportunities and diminish the quality of their choices to build a better life.[5] Racial inequality manifests in Black communities today, and it shapes conditions and opportunities for learning throughout students' schooling.

Relative to all other racial groups, Black undergraduate students are the second largest group of Federal Pell Grant recipients, a measure for financial need.[6] At 46 percent, nearly half of all Black undergraduates hail from homes and families that qualify them for the highest levels of federal financial assistance. In 2014 a staggering 39 percent of all Black children under the age of 18 lived in poverty, a 5 percent increase from 2007.[7] In contrast, during the same five-year period, White children living in poverty increased by 3 percent. Concentrations of poverty in Black communities are largely found in urban regions of the nation, partly due to a scarcity of employment opportunities.

Changes in the workforce and an unease with growing African American populations in cities pushed many middle-class White families to leave cities for more affluent neighborhoods, or what we know as "White flight," which left urban regions starving for a prosperous future.[8] Many Black families, without similar resources, were unable to take flight. As industry moved away, families found themselves in neighborhoods with high unemployment, which crippled their communities. In fact, Blacks are twice as likely to be unemployed than Whites, a pattern that has persisted for the past six decades.[9] Coupled with the poor regulation of fair housing laws in the 1960s and 1970s, the remnants of rampant residential segregation amplified the concentration of poverty, exposing residents of poor neighborhoods to increased violence and danger.[10]

Although residential segregation is no longer legal in the United States, it persists to the present day and negatively shapes the daily lives of Black students and their families. Blacks are more likely to live in racially segregated neighborhoods, which are prone to higher levels of crime and poverty, which further reduce residents' employment opportunities and ultimately their potential to improve their economic and social status.[11] These conditions can take a negative toll on children's emotional well-being, creating stress and anxiety that lead to poorer health outcomes and educational performance. Even in school, Black youth find the same forces diminishing the quality of their educational experience. The boundaries that define school districts mirror the very county lines that sort students by race and social class.[12] These boundaries have adverse effects on school funding, where students from less affluent neighborhoods are restricted to schools with limited financial resources and hence fewer developmental opportunities.

The structure of family life also has serious and long-term consequences that can determine the quality of a student's educational trajectory.[13] Black student achievement is shaped by the components of this structure, including the presence of parents and the quality of their investment in cultivating human, cultural, and social capital. In a national study of the social origins of students attending the nation's most elite colleges and universities, survey respondents reported that by the time the child reached six years of age, Black mothers were twice as likely to work full-time compared to Whites, Asians, and Latinos, and Black fathers were more likely to be absent in their children's lives.[14] This can leave a small balance of time to fully cultivate the values, dispositions, and skills that are often required to succeed in school. For instance, Black parents were 20 percent less likely than White parents to read to their children, and 9 percent less likely to take them to theatrical plays and concerts. Unequivocally, we know that early exposure to reading, especially in the home, has significant and positive effects on student literacy outcomes, and that strong reading skills can help students build on their achievements in school and later in life.[15] Black parents are also less likely to expose their children to events and activities valued by educational institutions. These include resource-driven activities such as cultural events and after-school sports, which can improve a child's ability to navigate colleges and universities that are built on specific middle- to upper-class and White cultural knowledge, beliefs, and attitudes.[16]

Racial differences in quality of parenting and parental involvement are largely due to structural circumstances that constrain a parent's resources, as well as different ways of parenting.[17] These differences, however, should not suggest that Black parents lack the desire to provide the opportunities that will maximize their children's progress on the pathway to college. In fact, Black parents are just as likely to value education and to report a desire to be just as involved with their children's education as White parents.[18] Among low-income Black families, it has been observed that parents with almost no experience with higher education are connected to a wide network of individuals from cultural resource centers, extended family members, and churches to gain access to information and resources to support their children's achievement and navigation through school.[19] These parents may not have the economic resources that traditionally advantage middle- to upper-class White families, but they are rich in the relationships that they develop and maintain throughout their community. Nonetheless, the positive relationship between a parent's level of education and the student's likelihood of graduating from college is well established.[20] Black students are less likely to have college-educated parents, placing them at a significant disadvantage compared to their peers with college-educated parents knowledgeable of the inner workings of college culture, such as identifying the criteria for admission, negotiating with school agents for resources to meet these criteria, and structuring their child's activities to optimize their chances of success. The difference between parents with and without experience in higher education can help explain why parents without exposure to higher education often assume that the high school is responsible for their child's educational trajectory, not realizing that their child's school may not have the resources to meet that obligation.[21] These circumstances generally are beyond a parent's control and unequally contribute to a student's path (or lack thereof) to higher education.

In the past forty years, there has been substantial absolute growth in U.S. minority college enrollment, which suggests, in part, that there have also been improvements in the conditions (throughout the preschool–12 pipeline) in which minority students prepare themselves for college.[22] This tendency to associate this achievement with improved preschool–12 conditions is not without serious flaws. More Black students are enrolling in higher education, but overall they continue to hail from poorer-quality schools, demonstrating that not all students begin college on an equal footing.[23] Students' performance in college is also largely determined by their peers, their access to advanced and rigorous college preparatory curriculum, and the quality of teachers and staff.[24] In other words, the distribution of educational opportunities before college operates as a sorter, determining who is and who is not college-eligible and college-ready. This is especially true for students interested in STEM.

Black students are more likely to graduate from the most disadvantaged secondary schools, measured by the percentage of students eligible for free or reduced-price lunch, as well as the percentage of students satisfying pre-college course requirements.[25] Meaning, Black students are more likely to attend a secondary school populated by students from families in financial hardship, which is associated with a shortage of experienced teachers and limited school resources to provide college preparatory courses.[26] Such conditions can worsen students' prospects of navigating the path toward entry into college.[27] The disadvantages experienced in high school may even erode the path toward graduation, especially in STEM. According to John Yun and José Moreno, "Without an equal starting line, such standards . . . may make the goal of universal access [to higher education] largely unattainable for those racial / ethnic groups faced with multiple disadvantages within their school settings."[28]

Negative Narratives

Pushing against the progress of Black communities in educational attainment are the negative narratives that have evolved across time to accommodate society's changing views on race and equality. Despite the election of the first Black U.S. president, Barack Obama, the media are laden with images and stories of Blacks as the underclass, residing in dilapidated neighborhoods while avoiding employment and exploiting social welfare services.[29] And most importantly, the poor conditions and violence that many Black Americans face are seen as their own doing, results of their supposed inherent unintelligence and lack of work ethic. In-depth ethnographic research on Black families and communities has demonstrated the falsity of these narratives by documenting the resiliency of Black individuals—in the form of maintaining key interdependent relationships among community and extended family members and doing the best with what they have—as a response to the structural conditions of poverty.[30] However, due to the disparaging social stereotypes Black students continually find their intelligence and admission to college questioned, which diminishes their sense of belonging in college.[31] Such prejudicial treatment is frequently reported as a significant force in shaping Black students' aspirations for and performance in STEM.

The influence of these narratives is far from harmless, as demonstrated by Jesse's story. Interviewed during their first year at the University of Virginia while enrolled in calculus, a course required for future STEM courses, Black students persistently reported negative interactions with non-Black students.[32] There were few Black students in large lecture halls, and these students believed that their non-Black peers possessed a negative perception of their performance, giving them bleak prospects for finding peers with whom to collaborate and study. Racial minorities also continue to encounter unfriendly faculty members, some of whom are blatantly racist. One national study reported that a Black male science major was told by his professor that he did not qualify for a research assistantship because the professor was searching for "somebody like myself."[33] Others reported faculty members being abrupt and rude with them while spending inordinate amounts of time with White and Asian students, populations with reputations for inherent intelligence and the capacity to learn and achieve in STEM.

What is most detrimental in the way stereotypes affect and shape student performance is the risk of students internalizing, or accepting, these messages as fact.[34] For instance, Black math and science undergraduates at the University of California at Berkeley reported that the primary reason for their poor performance in STEM was their lack of intelligence.[35] Some Black students have been made to believe that they were admitted to college only for reasons of affirmative action, and not for any talent or ability that warranted their admission.[36] The internalization of these messages can erode their confidence and lead students to justify their departure from math and science by redefining their perception of these fields as irrelevant to their daily lives. However, the influence of these negative narratives and stereotypes is not fixed or guaranteed.[37] Certainly, students receive all kinds of messages from their peers, faculty members, campus staff, and family. In a study of high-achieving African Americans at a PWI, students claim that the positive messages from family members and friends from home were motivating factors to persevere in spite of the challenges encountered in their STEM classes, deflecting or reducing the influence of narratives and stereotypes.[38] Other Black students, though, can be overwhelmed by the fear that their performance will confirm the negative narratives and stereotypes. Such fear can undermine their performance and their expectations for the future.

Researchers Claude Steele and Joshua Aronson labeled this problem "stereotype threat" and conducted several experiments to determine the degree to which Black student achievement could be explained by students' inherent ability or their fear of confirming societal stereotypes.[39] They hypothesized that notions of racial inferiority negatively fashioned how students perceived themselves as not belonging in college or in White, male-dominated fields of study. Compared to White students in the study, Steele and Aronson found that Black students underperformed when placed under "diagnostic" conditions. When conditions were altered to present a non-test-like environment, Black and White students performed similarly, suggesting that the fear of confirming the stereotype of academic failure was present for Black students. Improving Black student achievement in STEM, and in higher education generally, has recently been a priority for some federal programs.[40] There have been investments in educational programs and services to improve Black students' preparation for, and increase their interest in, STEM, but little consideration has been given to helping students navigate the competitive STEM culture that promotes stereotype threat.

More recent work has looked at how altering the environment can mitigate or minimize the racial gaps—related to stereotype threat—in achievement. In their study of African American achievement in college, Catherine Good, Joshua Aronson, and Michael Inzlicht conducted an experiment to help students resist the effects of stereotype threat.[41] The study included 79 undergraduates: 42 Black and 37 White. All of the students were given several messages over the course of a semester that encouraged them to consider intelligence as malleable— as a muscle that grows with hard work—instead of seeing it as a fixed attribute. Compared to White students, Black students had the greatest gains in GPA, which suggests that the messages students receive from their environment can deflect the influence of racist stereotype narratives. The findings in this study and others confirm that stereotype threat can be reduced by altering students' environments or reframing the activities that traditionally advantage White students.[42]

College Readiness

Several factors constrain Black students' abilities, chances, and opportunities to succeed in a STEM degree program. Unequal access and achievement in college preparatory courses bear significantly on students' intentions to major and persist in STEM and on how well students in high school can shape their chances for success in college.[43] At the college level, in the field of STEM, this is certainly true. Preparation for college-level math and science can include enrollment in algebra I, geometry, algebra II, trigonometry and math analysis, calculus I and II, biology, chemistry, and physics.[44] Students completing the highest levels of math are more likely to succeed in their college courses. For instance, in explaining how well students' performance in high school physics conditions their performance in introductory physics during the first year of college, Philip Sadler and Robert Tai found that enrollment in general high school physics had significant, but modest, association with students' final grades in introductory college-level physics.[45] The association was stronger for students who had taken an advanced physics course. A more recent study related to students pursuing engineering similarly found that students enrolled in AP physics and calculus achieved higher grades in the STEM gateway courses.[46] Achievement in high school calculus also predicted achievement in physics I, physics II, and calculus II. Students who have access to, and enroll in, the appropriate math and science classes are priming themselves for the rigor of college-level STEM. But access to these classes is not equal across races and social classes.

Minority college students, on average, are less academically prepared than White males.[47] Recent data from the U.S. Department of Education indicate that many Black high school students are not sufficiently prepared for college-level courses in STEM.[48] In 2009, across private and public high school students, enrollment in algebra II was relatively equal for Blacks, Whites, and Hispanics: 70 to 77 percent of each population were enrolled in algebra II. Considering that algebra II is the minimal level of mathematics a student must achieve to qualify for admissions to college, these are promising statistics. However, additional math is usually required and preferred to indicate readiness in pursuing a STEM degree pathway.[49] Once students pass algebra II, there is a significant drop in enrollment in more advanced mathematics across races, with the largest reductions occurring in the Black and Hispanic student population. White enrollment from algebra II to analysis / precalculus dropped nearly 40 percent; Black student enrollment dropped 47 percent. At the calculus and calculus Advanced Placement / honors levels, these disparities in enrollment are even more troubling. Of White students, 17.5 percent were enrolled in calculus and 11.5 percent were enrolled in calculus AP / honors; of Black students, those percentages were only 6 percent and 4 percent. Lastly, students are usually required to take the biology, chemistry, and physics sequence in high school to satisfy STEM course prerequisites in their first year of college. Black students are 10 percent less likely than White students to satisfy this course sequence, with similar patterns of distribution in the Advanced Placement / honors-level science courses.

Based on these disparities in enrollment, one can deduce that Black students are not entering college with sufficient preparation to optimize their chances for success and further opportunities in STEM. Moreover, several studies discovered that enrollment in these courses can improve student intentions to pursue, and persistence in pursuing, a STEM degree.[50] For instance, Catherine Riegle and Barbara Crumb found that when academic background was held constant, Black males were more likely than White males to declare a major in physical science or engineering.[51] Unequal access to and enrollment in the proper high school STEM courses reduces Black student STEM performance in college.

The First Two Years of College

Despite minority students' intentions to pursue a STEM degree being comparatively equal to those of Whites, departure rates from STEM are highest during the first two years of college for minority students at four-year institutions.[52] Minority departure from STEM is encouraged by negative experiences in the gateway courses, where the culture emphasizes grades over learning and a competitive "weed out" climate, undergirded by unsupportive faculty members and peers.[53]

What are gateway courses? To earn a degree in any of the STEM fields, a sequence of classes is required before students can enroll in upper-division, major-specific classes. The content in each of these courses is considered a platform of knowledge upon which students build as they progress in their major. There is a wide array of courses that are considered gateway courses, but for our purposes we focus on those commonly required for all students choosing to declare a STEM major: college algebra, precalculus, calculus I, II, and III, statistics, introductory biology, general chemistry, organic chemistry, introductory physics, and introductory computer science.[54] Students' interest in STEM is particularly high in the first year of college. If their performance in the prerequisite courses is unsatisfactory, students can lose their drive and fail to pursue or progress in their STEM major and ultimately lose access to subsequent opportunities. These prerequisite courses are considered the "gateway" to such opportunities. Racial and ethnic minority students disproportionately underperform at this stage of the STEM pipeline and leave behind their aspirations for a STEM degree.

According to the National Academy of Sciences, "introductory science courses often give undergraduates their first, and for many students, their last formal exposure to a deeper understanding of science. . . . Students often decide whether they will major in science on the basis of their experiences in introductory courses."[55] Performance in the gateway courses has a meaningful influence on minority students' path to a degree. Using a database of 15,000 students across the University of California and California State University systems, Charles Alexander, Erica Chen, and Kevin Grumbach discovered that Black and Latino students were less likely than White students to earn an A or a B in gateway courses. For example, compared to 65 percent of Whites, 29 percent of Blacks and 36 percent of Latinos received an A or a B in biology.[56] Racial disparities in achievement in the gateway courses could not be explained by minority students' poorer secondary academic preparation, which was measured by GPA and SAT scores, suggesting that factors in college were the primary culprits. And compared to White and Asian students at Stanford University, Black and Hispanic students showed the largest decline in interest in pursuing the premedical path due to negative experiences in the chemistry sequence and poor academic advising.[57] As reflected in this evidence, not only are minority students underachieving in the gateway courses, their underperformance is discouraging them from persisting in STEM. These findings suggest that "there are factors operating within the college environment itself that may contribute to the lower grade achievement of underrepresented minority students in [the gateway] courses and that these differences in academic achievement in college are not fully attributable to disadvantages experienced in the precollege states of the educational pipeline."[58]

Studies attribute the underperformance of minority students in the gateway courses to a culture of science that is structured to advantage individuals amenable to competition. For instance, Elaine Seymour and Nancy Hewitt documented how faculty members on the first day of class would assure students that many of them would buckle under the pressure and challenges of the course, suggesting that not all students could be successful in the sciences.[59] Another study reported that minorities found the competitiveness of their peers in the gateway courses to be "negative and disempowering."[60] Minority students interpret this experience, which is compounded by an unwillingness of majority students to share resources and study together, as a measure of their potential in STEM.[61] Recall Jesse's treatment by other students when she asked to join a study group. Conversely, another study found that students who were in classrooms where faculty members dispelled notions of competition were more likely to maintain their interest in science, despite the challenges they experience in the gateway courses.[62]

Challenges to Black student achievement in STEM emerge from much larger, systemic barriers that shape the quality of education provided and the ability of students to learn what they need to prepare them for success in college. But even then, college itself and the prevalent culture of STEM—individuality, the myth of meritocracy, and the value of competition—present a series of roadblocks that amplify the effects of racism and poverty that students overcame to be admitted to college. Despite the larger message of equity and opportunity coming from our country's leading institutions, behind their walls and inside their classrooms, their organizational ethos remains steeped in unquestioned norms and practices and long-held beliefs in minority student inferiority, reproducing racial inequality in the broader American society. There are solutions, however, that all institutions can consider if they are serious about eradicating racial disparities in STEM.

2

Institutional Responsibility

IN THE WORDS OF HENRY TISDALE, president of Claflin University, "You have to believe that students come in with potential and that they can be successful. Then, you must have a faculty member who is committed to working one-on-one with students and helping them through difficult times, or maybe not letting the students opt out." These words capture the first dimension of making Black scientists: institutional responsibility. Enacting institutional responsibility to promote Black student achievement in STEM is rooted in the belief that *all* students have the inherent intelligence and capacity to learn and succeed no matter their circumstances. It is the responsibility of faculty members, staff, and administrative leaders—the institution—to acknowledge these circumstances, to positively shape students' vision for the future, to supplement and enrich students' prior academic experiences, and to support students in their ability to balance the rigors of college and personal life. In working with students, said President Tisdale, "You've got to be willing to give them the support that they need." This chapter focuses on what that "support" looks like, because expecting students to conform to the narrow set of standards and norms commonly held by colleges and universities can undermine their achievement. We first explore what it means when colleges and universities acknowledge and understand their students, which then leads to how this knowledge is used to shape how faculty and staff support students both inside and outside the classroom.

American higher education was founded at a time when only young White men from elite families were considered deserving of an education that would maintain or elevate their standing in life.[1] Institutions of higher education were created to cater to and privilege students from these backgrounds to ensure their success and to justify their status in society. Despite the progressive evolution of higher education, mirroring America's broader embrace of equality and opportunity and widened college access for students of all racial and social backgrounds, we can still see today in our colleges and universities the consequences of their origin.[2] To this day, colleges and universities—in their expectations and assumptions regarding college readiness, student finances, student learning, student engagement, and student commitment—continue to privilege White students from well-to-do backgrounds, which creates conditions that discourage students from diverse backgrounds.[3] What can be done?

Broadly speaking, colleges and universities are responsible for providing space for students to explore, opportunities for students to realize and cultivate their potential, and faculty members to expand students' knowledge of the world, but they often fall short of fully committing to student success when it entails addressing the challenges that disproportionately affect minority or low-income students.[4] Students are expected to actively take advantage of available opportunities and resources to pave their own pathways to success. Our research with ten HBCUs taught us that transforming student aspiration into achievement in STEM requires that institutions—the faculty members, staff, and senior leaders—recognize and embrace the realities of their students in their daily practice and meet students "where they are" instead of expecting them to have the resources, know-how, and vision to succeed on their own.

Enacting greater institutional responsibility, or going beyond what is normally expected of colleges and universities, requires recognition that students' confidence and college know-how vary greatly by race and socioeconomic status. Some students enter college less academically prepared for the curriculum and how professors teach it. Some students have a difficult time envisioning how to achieve their academic goals because they do not personally know anyone who attended college. Some students have obligations outside of college, such as work and family, that make it difficult for them to have the time and focus needed to earn a degree in STEM. Institutional responsibility is understanding the circumstances that can constrain student progress and taking action to mitigate their influence, particularly with regard to students who need greater attention and support.

Acknowledging and Knowing Your Students

In meeting with faculty members, staff, and administrators at the HBCUs, it became apparent to us that getting to know their students well was crucial to their work. This meant understanding how the nuances of students' lives shape, promote, and constrain their ability to pursue a STEM education. This was not easy, and it normally took more time than many faculty members expected. The degree of such effort is characterized by Morgan State University faculty member, Professor Barry Wilkins, as a "labor of love." When time is dedicated to engaging with students to understand the relationship between their lives and their potential for success in college, institutions can begin to alter the pathway for students from disadvantaged backgrounds.

At Cheyney University, faculty members spoke about the hardships that overwhelm their students' commitment to achievement in STEM. Earning a STEM degree often symbolized an opportunity to be leaders in their community, to make a broader and more meaningful impact on the world, but those aspirations are hindered by the distractions of their home life, prior negative experiences in school, and lack of personal acquaintance with others who have achieved the levels of success the students aspire to.[5] Countering these influences requires faculty members to see their students beyond the common, negative narratives society tends to hold about Black students.[6] When asked how faculty members get to know their students, Greg Reid, a chemistry professor at Cheyney, explained his approach as a matter of fact: "At most HBCUs, the teachers tend to know the student by name, or if not by name, by some characteristic that the student is proud of. They're an athlete or fraternity guy or in the band or whatever, and they make it known this is what they value. . . . They are not invisible here." Reid's response speaks to the greater concerns and challenges related to race in American education. Black students are often victims of stereotypes and biases that negatively shape teachers' assumptions about their potential, intelligence, and capacity to thrive, and that render them "invisible" in the eyes of educators.[7] At Cheyney University, they are made visible and understood by "some characteristic" or point of pride and not by the biases linked to the color of their skin. Knowing student names, and taking the time to associate students with their talents and strengths, are some ways that faculty members acknowledge students and inform them that they are valued in the college community. It was this level of acknowledgment that persuaded Michael, a junior studying biology, to attend Claflin University. "They were the ones who just stayed on me. They wanted me. I wanted to go where everyone knew my name."

Once this relationship is established, this level of recognition lays the groundwork for cultivating student success, as explained by Professor Reid from Cheyney University:

> It's incumbent upon teachers . . . at HBCUs to have high expectations of the students despite what they may think the students' individual weaknesses may be. If they don't expect high expectations, they don't get them. If they think the students can't learn, the students don't learn. If they think they can, students will take every opportunity to show you that they can.

Improving students' chances of success in STEM is contingent upon faculty members believing that students can achieve. Faculty members must see inherent promise in students. Made visible by this acknowledgment, students can demonstrate "that they can do the work." If faculty members do not express high expectations for their students, "they don't get them," meaning the importance of believing in students' inherent intelligence and capacity to learn is undergirded by the expectation that students achieve no less than what their potential allows for. This relationship between faculty members' perceptions and students' actions is crucial to how we think about promoting the success of students. Opportunities are valued and taken when students' own confidence in their abilities is supported by the assurance and confidence conferred by their faculty members. Colleges and universities can continue to financially invest in providing more opportunities for students, but before these opportunities can be accrued, a fundamental step must be taken—faculty members must actively acknowledge students and their potential to succeed.

Acknowledging students' inherent ability to achieve is a meaningful first step in taking responsibility for their success. But to be clear, making students feel visible—knowing their names and having high expectations of them—does not mean ignoring the social realities of home life that continue to influence students' experiences in STEM. Quite the opposite. At Claflin University, faculty members and administrators frequently spoke of the communities their students come from, areas once thriving with industry that are now drained of economic resources, when explaining the challenges students confront in STEM. Professor Marion Greene, dean of the School of Natural Sciences and Mathematics at Claflin, explained:

> It's not that they're incapable . . . but they haven't been exposed. When they're in high school, they don't necessarily go to the best high school, because a lot of them come from the so-called South Carolina "corridor of shame," where the schools were neglected as it relates to having the kinds of facilities that they needed, books that they needed. For example, you have schools in which they don't have enough books to give all the students.

Believing in students' inherent ability to succeed and the institution's role in fostering it is to realize that their educational path to date is primarily shaped by forces *beyond* their control. In the case of Claflin students, they may have begun their tenure in college at a real disadvantage because of their home background—students who had attended less-resourced secondary schools in the "corridor of shame" did not receive the quality of education and experiences commonly expected of students when entering college.[8] As a faculty member for nearly twenty years at Claflin, Greene was quite in tune with the challenges her students frequently face:

> We know that these students are capable of learning. It's just that they've not been exposed or they've not had the facilities that allow them to get what they needed. So, once they get here, we understand that we have to teach [when students] come through the door. And by teaching those individuals that come to the door, we meet them where they are. And when they leave here, they can go to places like you see up there on that board.

The board Greene refers to spans the wall of the office where we held our meetings with faculty members and staff. It holds the names of prestigious universities and global Fortune 500 corporations in which Claflin STEM graduates have either been offered admission to or hold positions. For Greene and her faculty members and staff, this list celebrates the achievements of their students, but it also reminds them who their students are and how far they—as faculty and staff—must go to "meet them where they are." At times this can require extensive questioning of what it means for students to be college ready.

Expanding the Notion of College Readiness

When students graduate from high school and enter college, they are supposed to be "college ready."[9] That is, students are believed to arrive at college sufficiently prepared—academically, emotionally, socially, and financially.[10] But in fact, admitted students can represent a wide range of academic preparation. Consider mathematics. Black high school graduates are 15 percent less likely than their White peers to have taken precalculus, a prerequisite for college calculus.[11] For Black students who did not graduate from high school with this course completed, either because it was not available or because they were never given the chance, this can delay their entry into a STEM degree program.

When we asked faculty members what common challenges students encounter in the gateway courses, they unequivocally focused on students' need to be brought "up to pace." HBCUs recruit students with a wide range of academic preparation, but many of these students enter college unprepared to handle the rigor of college-level science and mathematics.[12] The quality of public education is often linked to zip code. Highly segregated and less-resourced neighborhoods tend to have poorer-quality schools and social services.[13] Faculty members across the ten institutions blamed an underfunded K–12 school system that failed to provide students with opportunities—as it relates to content and study skills—that would help student succeed in college. Professor Byron Hill, a faculty member in the department of biology at Prairie View A&M University, summed it up: "The public school systems. They're lousy."

Students can have difficulty with the college-level fundamentals in biological and physical sciences because they were not adequately educated in the prerequisite knowledge. Professor Wendy Lee, a biology faculty member at North Carolina Central University, elaborated on this point: "They've missed the fundamentals of just a basic scientific method from third grade on, just basics about scientific discovery, just basics about botany, plant life, just some of the basics." Lee emphasized how the state failed the students who enroll at North Carolina Central. Four-year institutions such as North Carolina Central award the baccalaureate degree to individuals who master the concepts in their disciplines and yet students without the basics enter college already at a disadvantage. At North Carolina Central, faculty members such as Lee must find a way to help their students make up for almost ten lost years of education. Eric Turner, a professor in the mathematics department, emphasizes a similar point:

> I find students, they can do, they can take the calculus part, they can take the derivative. But once they get the derivative, sometimes they can't do anything with it because they're so weak in the algebra. And I think some of that comes from, it's sort of like a rolling wheel. They miss out in high school, the lower levels. When they get here, we're trying to also get them up to speed to do the algebra, and sometimes trying to do that in one semester, two semesters, it's just not going there, or they can learn how to do it long enough for that class, but can they carry it over to keep it going?

Even when effort is exerted to bring students up to speed, how much of it will last? The K–12 years are a long period of time in which students who are provided with good educational experiences can build on their knowledge and practice and advance their mastery of core concepts. Many of the students attending the HBCUs in this study were not given those opportunities during the K–12 years. Faculty members may spend the additional time teaching the fundamentals, which, according to Turner, could improve a student's success rate in a given course, but there is little guarantee that the challenge of an academic deficiency would not come up again, especially in upper-division courses that assume a certain and sustained level of knowledge and skills. The underwhelming preparation students receive at the K–12 levels is akin to a "long shadow" cast upon their lives—it continues to nip at students' achievement no matter how far they travel.[14]

From our discussions with faculty members, it was quite clear that many of their students did not meet the traditional standards of college readiness for the pursuit of a STEM degree. But for these faculty members, that did not matter. Enacting institutional responsibility means that faculty members and staff take an active role in helping—elevating—students to reach that standard. In the words of Professor Harold Cooper, an associate dean of engineering at Morgan State University,

> We get students here who come in and the highest math they might have taken might be tenth-grade algebra, and they want to be an engineer. The question is, how do you take that person from that background and that preparation and nurture them, mentor them, and keep them engaged so that by the time they graduate from an accredited program, they are as well prepared and as confident as the other students who can come to the other big schools?

At Morgan State University, students can choose to pursue a major in engineering regardless of the level or quality of their math background.

When they enter Morgan State, all students are required to sit for a placement exam that will measure their level of readiness for college-level mathematics, normally calculus. Understanding that results from placement exams can underestimate students' actual competencies and therefore place them in courses further behind than they are in actuality,[15] Morgan State created "Foundations of Mathematics" (FOM)—an online, intensive, four-week course developed to promote students' confidence and their highest possible placement in college-level math and to minimize students' time to degree. The program coordinator and engineering instructor for FOM, Professor Richard Barnes, elaborates on the implications of enrolling in this program, especially for students without strong backgrounds in mathematics:

> Some of these students, the last math class they ever had was in tenth grade, maybe eleventh grade. They're all going to fail that placement exam, and they're all going to start at the lowest-level math, which is basic math. That's the stuff you teach in tenth grade and ninth grade, and a lot of students quit because of frustration. They say if I'm way down in my math curriculum, and they look at the curriculum and the first class we accept is calculus 1, and they see three classes between calculus 1 and the class they're taking, a lot of them just quit before they even get the chance to start doing any engineering classes.

Providing students with the opportunity to enroll in FOM is an example of "meeting students where they are." It is an opportunity that is less interested in student deficits and more about building upon what students already know and possess. FOM acknowledges students' backgrounds and is a form of action to help students better realize their aspiration to earn a degree in engineering. And part of this effort is helping students reconcile their perceptions of distance between where they currently are academically and what they must accomplish, to encourage them to move forward. Programs like FOM aim to minimize moments of "frustration," in order to minimize the possibility of students saying, "I'm not good enough," and quitting.

Across the four weeks, Monday to Friday, students in FOM are expected to dedicate two hours a day to their online lessons. These lessons respond accordingly to their math background in high school, which determines the content and pace of the course. Students, however, are not alone in this endeavor. Barnes explained how these lessons are supplemented with in-person and online support:

> On Saturday mornings, we have review sessions where they come to campus once a week, where we have tutors and mentors who work with them for about three hours. During the first hour and a half, they go over problem sessions. They go over any questions that they might have. They can still email the questions through the week. We have students who work with them, but the main face-to-face is on Saturdays from 9:00 A.M. to 12:00 P.M. Once they're done with their review, we give them a weekly test to figure out what they've done that week, and then we'll move on to the following week.

Designed to be highly flexible and adaptable to student needs and backgrounds, FOM does not fall short in meeting students where they are. Understanding the variability of students' schedules, FOM provides "tutors and mentors" to check in with students, to review the material together, and to provide real-time assessment of their progress. Reflecting on how participating in FOM affected his first semester, Lawrence, a Morgan State freshman in engineering, shared:

> For me, I definitely felt more confident going in. I learned some of those things in high school, but it kind of brought back the basic things I needed to know in order to do good. I felt like I got in a good place where I needed to be at, and [FOM] kind of reminded me [what] I needed to know. I was confident going in where I was at.

This level of commitment is what it takes for engineering faculty members at Morgan State to elevate their students to a level required of them to be successful engineers. In elevating students to a level of readiness, it is imperative for faculty members and staff to widen their definition of this notion, for it may help capture and support more students in pursuit of a STEM degree.

Questioning "college readiness" also translates to how faculty members make sense of their teaching. Terri Parker, a professor of physics at Cheyney University, recognized that many of her students "were not well-prepared for college," and this made her realize that one "can't assume students will know certain things" and that teachers "have to put some effort into figuring that out and how to modify [their] classes." This has made her more intentional about the ways in which she presents the content. For example:

> I will give them stepping stones because when I came and started to teach, I would lose them in the first few weeks . . . I try to add different things. I added online homework, and

then tried to do more problems in class instead of just lecture and give them problems. Also, I see that students [are] not used to retain[ing] concepts . . . , so I will tell them to prepare a concept book right from the beginning—you write down the main concept of every chapter, and then I will let you use it for some of the tests and quizzes.

Teachers modify their procedures for all kinds of students, not just for those who are less academically prepared. But when Parker first began her faculty post at Cheyney University, the wide range of student backgrounds encouraged her to think strategically about how she was going to effectively reach her students. Adding "different things," or providing diverse avenues for students to understand the material, demonstrates a sensibility toward students who are not receptive to traditional modes of teaching (i.e., lectures) and have not been given the opportunity or time to learn fundamental concepts that are commonly expected of "college ready" students. To address this gap in knowledge, Parker requires her students to develop a notebook that highlights the main ideas from every chapter, a tool to reinforce their learning of core concepts needed for advanced study in STEM. Because her primary course—Introduction to Physics—is a prerequisite for STEM majors, Parker's efforts are critical in minimizing gaps in knowledge, or bringing students up to speed, before they face greater challenges in more advanced STEM coursework.

Part of the challenge of bringing students up to speed is also the false assumption that their time and energy can be completely dedicated to their academics. For faculty members in our study, providing and reinforcing core concepts in math and science required them to reconcile the extraordinary obligations that students manage outside of school. At Morgan State University, Daryl Roberts, professor of engineering, described the nature of these challenges:

> I've seen some situations with [students] where they only have a single parent, and the single parent that is with them is either on drugs or something like that. They come tell me, "My mom spent all my money last night that I was supposed to pay my tuition with or buy my books with," and that's serious stuff, not an excuse. Some of these kids, what they walk through every morning to get to school, I really give them credit, and I see the stress firsthand.

The degree of influence that students' background and home life have on their progress in STEM does not diminish their aspirations for college, but it can amplify the academic challenges that students experience in class. To ensure their well-being and their progress in their learning, Roberts would find resources on campus "to get them off the street or at least act as a broker."

Professor Reid, at Cheyney University, has taught an increasing number of students who struggle with the course material because they are dealing with a set of home-life circumstances that negatively shape their sense of self and make them question their ability to persevere and achieve. These circumstances include "their personal problems" or "family drama." "The majority of our students come either from Philadelphia or Coatesville or Chester and still have family obligations in addition to classwork, which puts an extra challenge on a lot of them." Proximity to family and home community have been found to be a key factor for some students in choosing their college, but it can also hinder their perseverance in STEM. The cities Reid mentioned are only 30 to 45 minutes away from Cheyney, close enough for individuals from students' home lives to overwhelm them with obligations that take them away from their studies. When this occurs, it can feel almost impossible to achieve a degree in a field that already requires so much of them. When Reid senses this struggle in students, he does not wait for them to seek support. "We find them and we hold their hands. We talk to them, [we] let them talk." For Kelli, a sophomore studying biology at Cheyney, Reid's teaching style spoke to her:

> If you really want to learn the material in this class, you're going to learn. He's going to send you podcasts. He's going to tell you to sign up for this, this video session. He's going to tell you to look at this lecture. He's going to have you take this quiz online. And then he's also going to make it fun.

Despite the challenges in her life that make it difficult for her to feel "very confident" in STEM, Kelli believes that if students express a desire to work hard, faculty members like Reid will find a way to support them. For Reid, pursuing higher education does not necessarily entail that students enter college detached from their prior life. It is a matter of accepting the fact that students who are "ready" for college might also be very much attached to their families and communities outside of college—these are not mutually exclusive.

How one acquires knowledge is equally important to the knowledge itself. Some students who were successful in high school find college to be a rude awakening. Underfunded K–12 systems can fail to give students opportunities to develop their critical thinking and study skills. Scott Baker, a professor of biology and animal science at Dillard, noted:

> Students come to college with the assumption that they can just memorize and that it's the critical thinking that is the

challenge. And so, what I see, and what I try to get the tutors to see, is that we have to make science relevant, and come alive, and show them that they really know so much of this because it is part of our everyday existence, but we don't realize it. And so, doing that and also getting them to understand, if you have to, this is like, you have to commit to the study, the number of hours we have to put in, maybe more than other courses, the practices there, the terminology is challenging. . . . If you're in here to make the commitment, then this is what we have to do. And for some of them the lightbulb goes on quickly, and some of them we kind of go around the mountain a few times before [it does]. But I think that the students, once they see that connection being made, then that's when we can see the success start to occur.

Students can gain new knowledge through rote memorization, but it may not be effective in helping students apply that knowledge to solve problems and make sense of new and more complicated topics in their courses in STEM, or what researchers call "meaningful learning."[16] Baker's concerns speak to how Scott and his colleagues structure their teaching and facilitate PASS (Peer Assisted Study Sessions), a mentorship program between younger and older students, who have a track record of achievement in the gateway courses.[17] Part of PASS mentors' responsibility is to show their mentees that college-level courses demand a different approach to learning, such as thinking critically and identifying how different concepts relate to "everyday existence," as opposed to rote memorization. Moreover, Baker points to the quality of students' study skills as a challenge to their achievement. A course in STEM can be a difficult endeavor that requires more hours to master the material, especially if students have not been exposed to more complicated scientific nomenclature. Because some students enter college with little awareness of the realities of college-level demands, succeeding in a course may also require these students to work harder to meet these expectations. PASS mentors can help facilitate their mentees' understanding of these expectations, as well as share strategies to meet them.

The frustration around the underpreparation of students rang loud and clear across the faculty members in this study, but this did not make them insensitive. Howard Griffin, a professor of anatomy and physiology at Prairie View A&M University, discussed his approach to this challenge:

> The mission of the university is to allow students an opportunity who might not have that opportunity at another institution. A lot of our students are coming in with some deficiencies and they need to be remediated. You must keep that in mind because you have to lecture or talk to your audience. You don't want to go in there and just talk above them because you'll see the lights just click off and they're looking elsewhere.

Bringing students up to pace means meeting them where they are. In this case, teaching students without regard to their background encourages little progress in their learning. In meeting with faculty members across the ten institutions, we conclude that they have a very sound and measured pulse on their students and the challenges their students grapple with daily. These pulses are very much considered during the management and implementation of STEM services because they inform how faculty members help students meet the expectations for achievement in STEM.

Reframing Narratives, Motivation, and Skills

Faculty members at the ten HBCUs also understand that students' circumstances include the systemic racism in our society that influences students' ability to envision their success in STEM. This racism manifests in the false narrative of Blacks' intellectual inferiority and in the unfair treatment of our Black students, and it continues to promote self-doubt in the lives of Black students.[18] Part of the institution's responsibility in addressing this barrier is to understand how these narratives influence students' learning and perception in STEM. Take, for instance, exams. Exams are used to assess students' mastery of the course content. They signal to teachers and to students how well or poorly they are doing. The fear of performing poorly, and thereby the fear of confirming a negative stereotype of Black intellectual inferiority—demonstrated by an exam—can cause students to perform well below what they are capable of doing. This process is an example of stereotype threat—in this case, exams threaten to expose and further reinforce the negative stereotype that Black students are inherently incapable of achievement.[19] Acknowledging how this false narrative preys on the confidence of Black students, Reid tries to reframe the use of exams in his classroom, "I've found that things like the concept of tests . . . I change it to opportunities. This is an opportunity for you to show me what you can do. Show me some skill sets. Where do you use this information?"

Rather than seeing "tests" as a measure of what they do not know nor understand, Reid wants his students to see his exams as opportunities to show what they do know, to demonstrate their strength with the material. That he asks his students to think of exams as opportunities assumes a possession, not lack, of knowledge. So often Black students are inundated with messages that question their ability and highlight their failures, while their accomplishments become exceptions and never the rule.[20]

In the effort to reframe students' perception of their own abilities in STEM and to counter those negative messages, it is important to find opportunities to celebrate their everyday accomplishments. This reminds students that they belong in STEM and have the capacity to succeed long-term. Reid elaborated on why this level of acknowledgment is important for his students:

> Give them a certification in every class they take, a certification that has nothing to do with the bachelor's degree . . . it's about someone else sees you and evaluates you and gives you a piece of paper that you can show mom. That gives them a lot of confidence to say, "Hey, I can now take this professor who is difficult."

One might see this approach as too much hand-holding, or coddling. For Reid, it is instead about conditioning students to believe in their own ability to learn and achieve. Students should not have to wait until they've earned their bachelor's degree to have this confidence, for they may need to improve their confidence much sooner. The pathway to a STEM degree and subsequent pathways after college, such as earning a Ph.D. or medical degree, are long and arduous and can require significant internal motivation. The people who are around them can cultivate this motivation in students.

In her teaching, Professor Parker sees the challenges students face associated with self-doubt and their continued questioning of their skills and ability to succeed, and how these can impede her students' daily progress. When asked what this looks like in her classroom, she offered the following example:

> Let's say I start going over problems . . . some students will say, "I don't get it, I'm confused, I'm confused." I say, "Stop saying 'confused.' When you say 'confused,' you're telling yourself you don't understand. Stop doing that and try to focus. Look at what is given. Look at the information, list the things that are given, the data given, and what you have to find. And then look up your formula sheet and try to figure out how to connect these. Stop saying 'I'm confused.'" And I must be very stern, otherwise they keep on saying that.

Motivating students involves far more than simply telling them that they have it in them to succeed. In Parker's case, it includes a constant set of reminders and instructions that challenge students' self-doubt and their doubting self-talk and that clarify a path for them to master the material. Parker instructs her students to stop describing themselves as "confused," to stop vocalizing self-doubt, and to "focus" and see that answering a problem is a matter of following a set of steps. They can then recast their statements as questions about how to handle specific aspects of a step in the solution procedure, instead of resorting to vague statements that seem to cast doubt on their intellectual abilities ("I'm confused"). Motivating students, then, does require encouraging them to persevere, but it also requires faculty members to establish a path for them to do so. Not doing so, to allow self-doubt and confusion to fester in students, can have grave consequences for how students choose to proceed in their journey to a STEM degree.

At Claflin University, faculty members and staff take a similar approach. Denise Williams, an administrator at the School of Natural Sciences and Mathematics, explained how they motivate students to overcome self-doubt and feelings of not belonging: "[We] involve them in different activities and let them know that they matter—in the things that we have planned for them, in the culture of the university, and the culture of the STEM—make them aware that they can make a difference, even though some of them may not have the best grades." Similar to Parker at Cheyney University, for Williams, motivating students to help them see beyond their self-doubts is to show them how they matter in the ways the institution is structured. Telling students to push through, to persevere, are empty words unless they are accompanied by tangible evidence that they belong. When we asked her to clarify what she meant by the "culture of STEM," she just pointed at the wall that listed all universities and corporations where students have landed during the summer or after graduation. That wall serves as a reminder to students that they are on a well-worn path, one that reflects that the university is built for *their* success in STEM.

Widening and shaping students' vision includes helping them understand that college requires new or strengthened approaches to being successful and cultivating in themselves the agency to motivate themselves and have a self-affirming perspective during times of struggle. Most colleges and universities tend to assume that admitted students are equipped to successfully manage this transition, that they can make sense of their new terrain and act in ways that best optimize their chances of reaching their goals. When discussing the challenges related to the transition to college, Daryl Roberts, a professor of engineering at Morgan State University, shared the following about his students:

> When they come in, many of them are excited to do science and engineering. They register, they take math courses. Some of them will face difficulty in getting a grade to move to the next math course. In other words, when they get to college, they're used to doing what they did in high school. You have to convince them that they have to do something different.

They must step it up, and we try to convince them that this is an environment in which you have to motivate yourself.

College can be a shock for students as the level and amount of work required of them tends to be higher and greater. They do not realize that the strategies that were successful for them in high school may be less effective in college. Roberts says that in addition to helping students learn the material so that they can progress to the next course, faculty members must also convince students that for their studies in college, they need to learn to do "something different," and help them understand the importance of cultivating self-motivation. This is an important skill because earning their degree can be an uphill battle—a path where they can sometimes feel alone, where all they might have to move them forward is their internal drive. At Cheyney University, Greg Reid uses students' moments of difficulty as opportunities to strengthen their capacity to handle and manage "discomfort" so that they leave college stronger than when they entered. When confronted with a student struggling in STEM, he responds:

> This is what an HBCU is about. It's about teaching you to be comfortable when you're uncomfortable. You're not even producing until you have that little space, that little room of discomfort, and that's where you should do your best work— when you're uncomfortable. Things that don't work are perfect for you. Now you can perform. You're going to be the person that's called upon when things don't work because you've worked in situations that didn't work and you made it.

Struggle and discomfort are not necessarily feelings to disregard and avoid. For Reid, as a faculty member, helping address those feelings means encouraging students to alter their perspective to embrace and learn from those moments. This is what psychologist Carol Dweck would consider fostering a "growth mindset." When students believe that they can cultivate the abilities to learn and navigate new social spaces, their academic performance and outlook on learning tend to improve.[21] Take Terrance, a sophomore studying biology, as an example. The transition to college included the challenge of "adjusting to different nationalities and voices" reflected in his faculty. It was not the material he found difficult, but the challenge of understanding and communicating with faculty members whose first language is not English. In his process of grappling with this challenge, he realized, "You've got to adjust the situation and adapt to it to be successful." Part of Cheyney's responsibility is to provide students—like Terrance—with experiences that will only build upon their strengths so that they are prepared for greater challenges that may lie ahead.

Lessons Learned

Improving the achievement and success of Black students in STEM takes an enormous amount of work and dedication on part of the institution and its faculty members and staff, because—simply put— Black communities continue to be structurally disenfranchised in every way possible.[22] This means that Black students, on average, report poorer educational outcomes than their other peers because of barriers including racism, poverty, and residential segregation.[23] What can continue to discourage Black student achievement is the enduring and stubborn culture of colleges and universities to privilege and value students that come "prepared" and "ready" to manage the challenges waiting for them in college. Not realizing this mismatch in what is considered college readiness can disadvantage students who are not from primarily White, middle-to-upper-class backgrounds, which makes earning a degree in STEM that much harder. We believe, however, that institutions committed to racial equity in STEM education should take a hard look at their own assumptions and practices—and perhaps, in doing so, look to HBCUs for inspiration. Here are lessons to consider when enacting greater institutional responsibility for student success in STEM.

First, get to know Black students, especially those who have already chosen to pursue a degree in STEM. Remember, aspiration rates are quite uniform across racial groups, but the persistence gap tends to widen unfavorably for Black students after their freshmen year in college. Learning students' names and their backgrounds and interests can help them feel "visible" and welcomed in a field that commonly discourages their achievement.[24] This approach can also help build rapport with students and encourage them to seek support when they need it the most.

Second, take hold of and question the assumptions institutions use to teach and support students. Being academically prepared and understanding how to navigate social spaces are skills not lost on Black students and other students of color; the narrow set of standards institutions use to form institutional expectations of students can often make it seem like these skills are unattainable. Earning a degree in STEM requires a handful of prerequisites that can keep students out. Often these courses are not accompanied by opportunities or additional resources from professors that understand and respect the differences in the quality of education their students have received in the past. The quality of preparation that students receive can be quite unequal. We suggest developing programming or curricula, like Morgan State University's Foundations of Mathematics program, to elevate students to the standard that is required of a STEM graduate. And with regard to teaching in the classroom, professors can work to understand that, because of variations in academic preparation, students might not all be receptive to a single mode or style of teaching. We also suggest pushing back against the notion of "full-time" student. In our study, student participants were full-time students, but they were also full-time brothers, sisters, sons, daughters, and partners—when institutions support students, it is important that students do not have to choose between their education and their home obligations. Faculty members can make a difference if they listen to students, talk to them, and provide them with what they need in terms of academic and social support so that they can better balance their responsibilities inside and outside the classroom.

Third, it is important to remember that some of the challenges Black students experience in STEM are linked to much broader forces beyond a student's control. Inextricably tied and overlapping consequences of an unjust—racist and classist—society, including poor academic experiences and lack of social and educational opportunities, take a significant toll on students' physical and emotional well-being and how students envision their academic paths.[25] Faculty members can foster improved learning through an understanding that false narratives and stereotypes of Black student inferiority in STEM can negatively affect how these students behave in class (e.g., they might not ask for help, or they might not speak up for fear of looking weak) and even who they get to work with—Black students tend to be a significant minority in STEM classes, and because of racial biases, non-Black students are less willing to work and collaborate with them.[26] Reaching out to Black students, or giving them more of your time, can help them feel that they are not in this alone. Because they can be prone to loneliness in STEM programs and must manage the challenge of addressing gaps in their fundamental STEM knowledge, Black students can face extra struggles on their pathways to STEM degrees. It is important to help students maintain their motivation by showing—not merely telling—students how to persevere, to learn, and to ultimately be successful. This can help them immensely in expanding their vision of a positive future. It is also important to help them become more self-sufficient in maintaining their internal drive and in developing perspective so that they can more effectively handle the challenges related to STEM and to their daily lives outside the classroom.

Many of these guidelines for developing institutional responsibility can seem overwhelming and even inefficient, given that faculty and staff must also attend to other responsibilities—other students, research, administrative tasks, and so on. Some institutions might not have abundant economic resources for planning and implementing new programs for Black students. Some institutions might seem constrained by antithetical cultural norms and competing needs and demands. However, we believe that no matter the type of institution and the responsibilities that faculty and staff may already have, institutions give up very little to actively reach out to Black students, as opposed to expecting students to reach out to them. Taking on the responsibility of addressing racial inequality in academic achievement requires institutions to look inward and determine how this task should be central to fulfilling their social purpose. Black students in STEM often experience a gap between what they know and have and what is unknown and expected of them in college. Institutions must be responsible for using their resources to fill that gap.

3

Peer-to-Peer Support and Intellectual Generosity

EACH YEAR ROUGHLY 35 PERCENT of freshmen enter college with the aspiration to earn a baccalaureate degree in a STEM area.[1] A series of challenges, however, can make it difficult for a student to transform their aspiration into real, tangible success in the form of class performance or degree completion. Black students aspire to earn a degree in STEM at rates similar to those of their non-Black peers.[2] However, four or five years after they enter college, a lower percentage of Black students complete a degree. Something happens between the time students enter college and when they leave. Of course, some students leave STEM programs because they have become more strongly interested in other courses and experiences. But there are day-to-day interactions between students that disproportionately sort students out of STEM. Reflect on the response Jesse received from her classmates when she tried to form a study group, and how it made her feel. Her classmates did not want to work with her because they believed she was intellectually inferior and feared that she would bring their grades down. She ended up completing her degree, but not without significant damage to her sense of belonging in STEM. Aside from the quality of preparation students received in their secondary school, the social conditions of their campus, including their interactions with fellow students, can influence their transition to college, how well they learn classroom material, and the decisions they make in achieving their goals. But what can happen for such students when they attend an institution that promotes an alternative academic climate that promotes their well-being? This chapter underscores the significance of peer relations and the positive benefits that students accrue when institutions promote a culture of collaboration.

During our visits to HBCUs, we found that students' perceptions of their peers were driven by collaboration, not by competition. So much of the research on the culture of STEM education in college characterizes the learning environment as competitive, independent, and self-directed.[3] These traits were also identified as the common reason so many women and students of color perform poorly in or leave the sciences—for these conditions can amplify feelings of loneliness and isolation that emerge from being a minority in a sea of White men. There is nothing wrong with being competitive, independent, or self-directed; when students find themselves out in the "real world," such attributes can effectively help them achieve their goals. However, any course in STEM undergraduate education that capitalizes on these traits only reinforces an exclusionary culture that advantages students who already possess the cultural know-how to meet its expectations. Our work with these ten HBCUs identifies a culture of collaboration that is best captured by a student's description of her own relationships with peers in STEM: "Your success is my success." When institutions such as those in our study promote the value of working together, they are suggesting that individual success does not emerge solely from individual effort—that effective learning is not necessarily a solitary activity, and that it is not true that individual students *should* themselves possess all the knowledge they need to best navigate their pathway to a STEM degree. The HBCUs we studied all promote and shape positive peer relations in their STEM programs. Their success in producing high numbers of Black graduates in STEM is partly due to their focus on helping their students cultivate community and encouraging them to care for each other's success.

Learning through Collaboration

In her second year, Carolyn transferred to Xavier University of Louisiana from an elite university on the West Coast. Her goal was to earn a degree in biology and attend medical school, and she had believed that attending the elite West Coast school would give her everything that she needed to achieve her professional dream. And coming from a long line of physicians, she had no reason to believe that her goal of becoming a medical doctor was out of reach. But her view quickly changed in her freshmen year when she began taking the first set of introductory STEM classes. Carolyn's high school prepared her well for the rigors of college-level science, but what she was not prepared for was the strongly impersonal nature of the classroom environment, which hindered her ability to perform at a level that met her expectations:

> I left [the elite private institution] because I was not satisfied with their science department. My biology classes, there were about 11 to 13 sections, 300 students in each section. They had 18 TAs assigned to each section. There was hardly ever any one-on-one time with my professor. The professors weren't even the people grading the exams. It was the TAs. And it just wasn't as hands-on as I wanted it to be. So, I made the decision after my freshman year that it's just not working. I made the decision to come to Xavier.

For many students, like Carolyn, Xavier has been *the* academic destination for achievement in STEM, largely because Xavier does not overwhelm its students with the enormous class sizes typical of larger universities, which can greatly reduce the amount and quality of attention given to students.[4] Nationally known for cultivating Black student success in STEM, Xavier's curricular and co-curricular approach is grounded in routine, practice, and a wide, tight network of support that include teachers as well as students. When it comes to helping students succeed in the gateway courses (the set of prerequisites for any STEM major in the first two years of college), Xavier addresses the challenge of the customarily high attrition in this early stage of the pathway through two distinct programs grounded in the value of collaborative, peer-to-peer support: drill instruction and the Chemistry Resource Center.

Lack of achievement in the general and organic chemistry sequences is considered a significant barrier to student progress in the sciences. Some consider these courses as the pivotal experience that "weeds out" the academically unprepared.[5] Through their curricular approach, Xavier incorporates drill instruction to rectify the inequalities in preparation their students received in secondary education. To earn a degree in a STEM area, students must have a minimal level of exposure to and mastery in the fundamentals of math and science, as well as the study skills to gain new knowledge in subsequent courses. Not all students enter college meeting these standards. Even students who were successful in high school encounter significant challenges in college, according to Lenore Campbell, a professor of chemistry at Xavier:

> We're very clear about whatever you did in high school, that's not going to translate to the same grades here necessarily. . . . We have charts—"This was your GPA in high school, this is your GPA at Xavier, and that means if you want that GPA that you had in high school, you're going to have to do more." And so, we try to be very up front—"This is college, this is very different."

Having "to do more" includes putting in greater effort to understand new "nomenclature" in college-level courses, developing new or improved study skills to adjust to different standards of rigor. High school GPA, although used as a metric to determine admission, is not an accurate indication of a student's potential.[6] Drill instruction provides all science students at Xavier with a structure for learning important, fundamental concepts in general and organic chemistry and for acquiring or refining study skills.

Drill instruction institutionalizes a highly regimented and required form of recitation, a supplement to the formal course lecture in which students are broken into subgroups and assigned to meet with a teacher's assistant at a separate time and space to clarify content discussed in class. At Xavier, drill instruction is led by students who have successfully passed the course. It takes place once a week for two hours throughout each semester. In each session, students

> do reinforcement problems. They turn [problems] in. They get immediate feedback of what concept [they] are not understanding before [they] move on to next week. The first hour, [they] just answer questions, their questions on what they struggled with. And then the second hour, they take a written test. We get [the tests] back to them by the next week. And so again they get immediate feedback of what concepts from this chapter [they] did not understand before it builds, because of course, [in] science, everything is cumulative.

This program encourages students to study each week, as the exams count toward their final grade, and offers them weekly insight on their strengths and weaknesses. In turn, it gives the student instructor an opportunity to monitor students' progress and provide additional support where needed. Unlike recitations at other universities, which are typically unstructured time for students to clarify concepts in the lecture with a graduate teaching assistant, drill instruction is "high touch" and regimented, proactively responding to student performance. Because there is little time before the next exam, participation in drill instruction encourages students to see studying as a process that needs to be broken down and closely managed—it builds study time into the curriculum. But the key ingredient that gives expression to the success of this program are the student instructors themselves, for they reinforce the concepts taught in the faculty lectures by explaining them in a more accessible manner, while also representing to other students evidence of their own possible achievement.

Student instructors inhabit a space that remains, at times, untouchable by faculty members, an area between student aspiration and student accomplishment. From the perspective of Dina Hunter, a chemistry professor, embedding a student as an instructor for drill instruction stems from faculty members' belief that collaboration among students is imperative to students' short- and long-term successes: "We try to foster the idea that you want to work in a group and help each other out, because that's what you're going to have to do in real life. If you're not going to be working by yourself, you need to learn how to interact with other people."

To see one's friend, or peer, in the position of instructor is both powerful and influential for how students effectively learn the material and perceive their own capabilities. Camila, a junior studying chemistry, reflected on her experience as a student instructor:

> I enjoy being a chemistry drill instructor. . . . As someone who completed the course, and did well in the course, I could shed light to some of the younger students . . . and it gives me a chance to mentor them as well, like they ask questions. Other than work, they want to know what it's like, how can they get through to the other side, and . . . it does take work, it takes a lot of work, a lot of studying, a lot of preparing . . . I just need to help y'all understand what y'all are doing and how to do it the correct way so that when you do see it again, especially on the exam, you don't miss it because it's something that, "Oh, I remember this from drill, this is how I worked it out in drill," and you can work it the same way on the test.

Camila comes off as experienced in the struggle of learning chemistry, as well as the benefits of being taught from a student instructor. She is privy to the feelings that younger students may be experiencing in general chemistry, but her success in the course sequence also gives her confidence in the advice that she gives. Faculty members can often give students similar guidance, such as "It takes a lot of work," but hearing this from a peer can give it greater legitimacy and substance. Ava, a junior studying chemistry, described the value in having a student teach other students:

> Chemistry is not easy in general. So, I feel like for Xavier to have students teaching them, they can relate on their level. Like for me, I have different tricks that the teachers don't have, because I learned it myself and I learned it in a different way. And I feel like that's really helpful, because . . . they may not understand their class. When they come here [drill instruction session], we kind of just break it down. It's helpful for them to have students helping them, their peers.

Ava's experience of overcoming the challenges in chemistry gave way to strategies that worked best for her and that she believed may be beneficial to students who may not grasp the concepts in the lecture. It is this level of knowledge and rapport with students that can help students translate their aspiration into achievement in STEM.

The influence of having a peer as an instructor has consequences for outside the classroom as well. Because students see their drill instructor every week, they begin to see other students as sources of meaningful support in their learning. Learning in STEM becomes less of a solitary act and more of a collaborative endeavor. Although Rachel, a junior studying chemistry, chose not to become a student instructor, she found the routine of working with her peers fruitful in subsequent courses: "Right now, I have group meetings with people from my metabolism class, and we'll set up a meeting time to go to the library and study together. So that's just our way of pushing each other, more so than anything else. More people are willing to work collaboratively more so than competitively."

Drill instruction is a mechanism that promotes long-term peer-to-peer collaboration. Xavier faculty members believe that collaboration is an essential study skill that they hope students will carry with them as they move forward in their STEM pathway, be it academia or in the STEM professions, all of which demand collaboration to achieve innovation. And because the students are working together, there is less of the competitiveness that is seen among other STEM departments across the country. The culture of collaboration encourages students to prioritize the academic well-being of their peers. Students discover that their learning and performance are optimized, not sacrificed, when working closely with others.

Furthering their efforts to ensure that students master the concepts of chemistry and are prepared for future coursework, Xavier established the Chemistry Resource Center. More than just a dedicated space for students to understand course content, similar to drill instruction, it centers student collaboration as the source for learning and for improving confidence in one's abilities. Every week of the academic year, Monday through Friday, students in general chemistry and organic chemistry are given all-day access to a dedicated space, including multiple whiteboards, where they can study or receive assistance from a peer tutor. In the words of Professor Bill Cole, a faculty member and administrator at Xavier, tutors are chosen from a pool of students who have performed well in their respective courses:

I wrangle a couple dozen smart, very smart, students. They all have an A in the courses that they're tutoring in, so they come highly recommended. They're strong in the subject matter. . . . The ones that I pick really have the spirit of intellectual generosity, and they don't mind giving what they know to help somebody else. And they also know, "Well, I've been here and done that, and so I can teach you how, especially freshman, how to do that and be successful." And I rely on that too because sometimes the kids just don't want to hear from the old guy in the room. I rely on the fact that the young patriots can tell them from their perspective in their own language, and tell them how to succeed, so it's a good system.

The Chemistry Resource Center is a system driven by a "spirit of intellectual generosity." The tutors not only must have achieved excellence in a given course, but they must also have a nature of being generous in sharing knowledge. This is essential, not only to the process of learning the content, but also to passing on the strategies and skills that have been effective in helping students succeed. In essence, the Chemistry Resource Center functions like a conductor, transmitting knowledge to every generation of STEM students. Cyndi, a junior studying chemistry, elaborates on this process of transmission:

> People that I've tutored have become tutors that I work with now. I help train tutors as well to have those same set of skills. And so, then they become my friends as well. So, they're in organic right now. Even though I don't tutor organic, I've been through organic, so they trust me to help them with organic. I live on campus, so they know where my room is, so they'll bring their friends or whatever to my room and we'll all just have a study session together, so I'll

help this corner with organic and this corner with general chemistry, and then they help each other. Once I teach—you know, help them understand—I make sure that they teach their friends. Instead of me teaching everybody, I tell them that once you understand it, you'll understand it better if you teach it to somebody else, so it kind of just trickles from there. You know, we try to work together to make sure everybody is on the same page, everybody is understanding the concepts. And if they don't understand it, they can feel comfortable to come to somebody like me or one of their friends.

There are many layers to this process, but they are all strung together by the value in helping others once students themselves have mastered the concepts. Cyndi is teaching others how to be tutors so that the transmission of knowledge can be successfully passed on— nothing is held on to and hoarded for individual gain or the improvement of only a small group of students. Neither Cyndi nor any other student becomes the only source of knowledge and support. By tutoring other students, Cyndi in turn is transforming her student colleagues into extensions of the resource center. And by encouraging them to tutor others, she reminds them that the act of teaching someone else can improve one's own understanding of the material.

At Lincoln University, incorporating supplemental instruction in the STEM gateway courses has improved student's understanding of the course material. Supplemental instruction is similar to drill instruction in its emphasis on peer-to-peer relations, but it is less structured and more focused on the transmission of knowledge. In supplemental instruction, a single student who has done well in the course is considered the supplemental instruction leader. For a stipend, the student leader attends all course lectures and hosts weekly review sessions for students in that given class. These review sessions offer students an additional opportunity to seek clarity in the concepts taught in class. This clarity comes from the manner in which the information is transmitted—peer to peer. For Trudy Bankmen, a professor of mathematics, supplemental instruction leaders are partners in teaching:

> Supplemental instruction is helping . . . because sometimes students communicate very well with students. They communicate very well rather than . . . I mean we try our best. We try to repeat. But sometimes they ask the best students or the SI leaders to speak out the way they will understand, it helps them. The SI leaders are the best students.

Stephen Cooper, also a professor of mathematics, chimed in:

> The supplemental instructors help keep the students exposed, beyond the classroom, to some of the material. Gateway courses—certain chemistry courses, physics, biology—you absolutely need them to move forward. And I think as much exposure as you can give for the students helps. . . . The supplemental instruction, I found it was really helpful, especially when you can find somebody you can work closely with. I've been fortunate in that one of my research students is my supplemental instructor. He knows me well, he knows what I want to do, he knows the material. I've just been fortunate, as it's been easy to communicate with him and let him break down what I want the students to know. And . . . sometimes I think the students can even relate to another student better than they can relate to me teaching them the material.

Both Bankmen and Cooper realize the importance of supplemental instruction because they understand that the vital material shared during lecture is not easily consumed. The student leaders are critical in this regard because the gateway courses are consequential to future achievement in STEM. By working closely with the professors, supplemental instruction leaders understand the aims of the lectures and can present them in their own style of communicating with their peers. Laurence, a junior studying biology, confirms Bankmen' and Cooper's opinions:

> I think SI is good. It helped me a lot. So personally, I like
> SI . . . I like it when I get there because I have students there
> who can help me, I like learning from my peers a lot. I like
> the group study. At times, I go to the professor, you have to
> book an appointment and stuff like that, and . . . she may not
> explain it to [you] the best. So, you want the peer to explain
> it to you the way they understand it, and you understand it
> better through that.

Despite the good intentions of professors to incorporate new strategies or innovations in curriculum and pedagogy, their presentation of the material in class may still hinder student learning, in part because no one method will account for the diverse ways in which different students learn best. Offering a program like supplemental instruction addresses the challenge of seeking support from faculty and provides students an alternative pathway to, for some, more comfortable conditions for their learning.

Through drill instruction, the Chemistry Resource Center, and supplemental instruction, Xavier and Lincoln focus on the role of peers supporting peers in student learning, which addresses both content and the skill of working with others to succeed. These structures have multiple benefits for students, including understanding and learning concepts in different ways, increased accessibility to support, and encouragement not to go down the path of "going it alone" and competitiveness.

Accountability through Collaboration

The first year in college can be full of distractions. Students are excited to be away from home, form new relationships, and, perhaps, make decisions free from the authority of or obligations to parents and families. The attraction of taking such liberties can make it difficult for students to maintain a daily routine centered on academic achievement in STEM—the adjustment to college life comes with the challenge of managing one's time and the responsibility to own one's work. Through the Premedical Concept Institute (PCI), a pre-freshmen summer bridge program, Prairie View A&M University helps students early on in this transition by providing a community for its STEM students that encourages students to keep a watchful eye on each other—to keep each other accountable for learning. Prairie View's approach is captured by the belief that personal success does not occur without the success of the community.

Considered a long-held tradition among current STEM students and alumni at Prairie View A&M University, the PCI has cultivated and graduated over 500 students in the STEM areas. These graduates have gone on to earn advanced degrees in the health professions, almost half of them having become physicians. A great deal of the PCI's record of success can be attributed to its founder, Professor Thomas Owens, and the younger faculty members he's cultivated to continue this work of improving student achievement in STEM. The PCI is a ten-week residential program during which students complete general biology I and II. Academic advising and structured community-building activities to help students acclimate to college life are included. The goals of the program are to reach out to students earlier to introduce them to other STEM students, cultivate their aspirations in STEM, and prepare them for the rigors of subsequent courses by giving them a head start on their gateway courses. This means that by the time they officially matriculate into Prairie View A&M University, they will have completed a year's worth of general biology, familiarized themselves with the intensity of effort it takes to study a STEM area, and developed a community of individuals dedicated to success in STEM.

Chris, a current freshman who recently completed the PCI, explained how it helped him make the transition to college:

> When I graduated high school, I graduated that Saturday and I had my graduation party Sunday and I was moving into my dorm that night. It [the PCI] was different. It really was. The biggest difference I would say is just the study skills aspect of it. I was talking to my parents and I was like, "I study more in one week than I did all four years of high school." Really. That's how different, just the studying, and then you learn how to study more efficiently. In high school, you might open your book, open up your notes, but then the TV is on and then your phone is here, and your game controller is here and everything. But in college if you do that, then you'll look up and you're like, "Oh my gosh, it's 3:00 in the morning and I haven't studied anything."

The intensity of the PCI programs offers little room for rest or "different distractions." Summer break can be a time to relax from the stressors of school, but it can also be a time where students' focus and discipline begin to wane, making it exceptionally hard to start a new semester. Participation in the PCI helps students maintain their academic momentum while encouraging sound time management skills. Students who watched TV every day in high school learn quickly that there is no time for it in college, where there is so much to learn in so little time. For PCI students, TV is a distraction not worth the sacrifice of their achievement. Students are learning that their time is precious, so it must be guarded. Bernice Woods, professor of biology, discussed how she helps students prioritize their studies in STEM: "All you've got to do is put a little time in. When you have the extracurricular activities that are put in front of you, think of it as this: The word 'extra' is there for a reason. That's not a part of your curriculum. That's extra. When you keep that in mind you will be successful."

Time management is a key element to achievement in a STEM field. STEM is a serious endeavor—a fact that the PCI and its faculties promote as truth on day one of the program. When students are confronted daily by a series of decisions regarding how to allocate their time, they are urged to prioritize their studies above all else. From Woods's perspective, anything "extra" should not be considered if it detracts students from their studies, which are first and foremost in deserving their utmost attention and focus. But the amount of work required and the encouragement from faculty members are not always enough. Students themselves play a significant role in keeping each other focused on their studies.

Being a member of the PCI community means that students spend a great deal of structured time with one another. A typical day includes almost eight hours of lecture and additional time for studying in the evening. Michelle is a sophomore studying biology, and for her, PCI was an important time to form relationships that can carry on and be beneficial in the long-run. Thinking back on her PCI experience: "The people that I met in PCI are great people to study with because they understand how you need to study, that [you] need to focus and they've been through everything with you, the long lectures and lab. So, they're great friends to make." Having friends with similar goals and sensibilities to achieving can be consequential to a students' ability to organize their time. In those ten weeks, the program offers plenty of opportunities in which students achieve and struggle together—these moments reveal how the relationships formed during summer lay the groundwork for them keeping each other accountable in future coursework. When we asked Michelle what "great friends" meant to her learning in STEM, she responded, "We all want everyone around us to be successful and I don't see why you don't want that." We found her response unexpected because the question emphasized only her performance, and yet her response spoke to belief that communal success leads to individual success.

A steward of this ideal is the founder of the PCI, Professor Owens. Tonya recalls the first week of the program and the advice Owens gave to the students: "We study together, and Professor Owens always said since you all are in PCI you'll have to stick together, you'll all socialize together. If you're somewhere, all you all should go together. Stay together, because that's how you're going to learn, because you're with smart people and you want to do things with smart people." The transition to college, a new environment, can present challenges to navigating new norms and rules, and learning two semesters' worth of general biology in ten weeks is no easy task. By encouraging his students to "stick together," Owens is asking his students to be there for and learn from one another. Since they have all chosen to participate in this program, they are considered smart—meaning, the choice to sacrifice one's summer after graduating from high school is an indication of their values, goals, and willingness to work hard. Lynne, a freshman, adds to the discussion about Owens and described what it means to "stick together":

> He establishes unity within the students. He always wants us to study in groups and work together and not compete for grades because there's no need to compete. Everyone can get an A. It's not like, "Oh, if I get an A, this person doesn't need to get an A." He's like, everyone can get an A. So, he establishes unity . . . knowing what you say might get out there to other people.

From Lynne's perspective, Owens prioritizes community among students. Because everyone holds some degree of knowledge, working with each other only maximizes everyone's opportunity to learn the material, as well as new skills to prepare them for the rigors of future coursework. Collaborating and working together can improve one's learning, which in turn could lead to earning high marks in the given course. Keeping knowledge to oneself does not advance the achievement of the individual or the community because each student can hold different and varying levels of understanding. This is why, for Owens, the concept of competition is irrelevant—it does little to encourage the success of all his students.

When students get together to study, their intentions are structured and precise. Will, a sophomore studying biology, told us that one has to "make sure that the people that you study with all have the same goals as you, [and] you just have to make sure that the people that you study with are there to study and not to have social hour. Study time is our time to study, get the material down. And then we can have so-cial hour." When students come together to study, the purpose of their time together is clearly delineated between learning and time spent socializing. But more importantly, the time together is inten-tional, so that "the people that you study with understand what's going on and you're not taking the time just sitting here trying to teach them everything. It's 'I'll show you this, okay, can you show me this.' It's that [back and forth] that helps us to learn more than just the one-sidedness of it." This level of community among students means that they are holding each other accountable. For someone like Chris, whom we talked about earlier in this chapter, his community with his PCI peers ensures that he is using his time efficiently. According to Chris, if he is not, one of his fellow PCI peers would make sure he does:

> Last year we used to probably be in the new science building
> around 7:00 or 8:00 at night to study, and we would all be in
> the same room. If somebody was missing, . . . we would text
> them, "Where are you? I think you're taking a nap, but I
> think it's time for you to get up." We would call them and
> be like, "Hey, get up!" and they're like, "No, I'm sleepy."
> We're like, "We don't care. You've got to get up!"

In talking with alumni from the PCI program, especially those in their second and third years at Prairie View, we sensed a strong degree of loyalty among them that was clearly formed during the summer before their first year. Chris's recollection speaks to how students conceive of their community, a stern unwillingness to leave anyone behind.

Giving students a head start on their STEM degree requirements, the PCI addresses the struggle of transition and community among new students. Similar-race working groups can improve student learning and performance in STEM, especially when students have similar academic goals, because they push back against a culture of STEM that is driven by individualism. Uri Treisman, an educational researcher and mathematics professor, had similar findings in his studies of Black undergraduates in mathematics almost thirty years ago.[7] However, along with its ability to bring students together with a common goal of achievement in STEM, what is distinct about PCI is how it cultivates a community in which students care for each other's learning and success. Throughout their time at Prairie View A&M University, working in a group was less a means to individual success than to communal success. Spending a concentrated amount of time together in the summer led them to carry these relationships forward in a manner that benefited how they structured their time and approached their studying. If any one student was slipping, the relationships formed through the PCI acted as a safety net, holding that student accountable and bringing them back into the fold.

Confidence through Collaboration

Danielle left her home state of California to attend Dillard University in New Orleans. During the time of our visit, she was in her last year of earning a degree in physics. Although she could have earned this degree closer to home, the experience of studying physics among those that understood and valued her background made a difference in her education:

> I think as African Americans we automatically feel comfortable when we're around our people. And like I said, in

California, Black people, we could sit in the same class-room and not even speak. And that's kind of like embar-rassing, you know, as to where here [Dillard University] they want to spread that tradition and teach other people. . . . I'm from California, so when I first got here I'm just like, okay, well I don't know if I should speak, I don't know. But the people from here make you feel comfortable with doing it.

Danielle's description speaks to a much larger challenge of how mi-nority students find comfort in a culture of STEM that is primarily dominated by White men. Dillard's success in graduating students in STEM, especially Black women in physics, can be linked to their Peer Assisted Study Sessions (PASS), which pair freshmen who intend to earn a STEM degree with a more senior student who has successfully completed the gateway course sequence common across all STEM fields. The senior-level students, or PASS leaders, are charged with holding weekly sessions to help their freshmen improve their under-standing of the course content by addressing first the issues related to the adjustment to college life. In contrast to the drill instruction at Xavier and the Premedical Concept Institute at Prairie View A&M, which were both primarily focused on helping students fine-tune their study and organizational skills, the PASS program is an intervention to mitigate the challenges associated with entering and navigating a new cultural space.

For freshmen with little knowledge or familiarity with the social landscape and academic demands of the university, a student mentor, or PASS leader, would be a welcome resource. As someone who is both a PASS leader and past mentee, Devon illustrates how the process built his own confidence so much that he is almost certain of the success of those he mentors:

> When I was a freshman here, I looked at the PASS leaders on campus and I thought that's who I want to be. And, leaders now that are graduating from here, they talk to me still today, and they always tell me that I'm thankful that I met you, and I'm very proud of you, and just always encourage me. So, whenever I tutor somebody, I can see where they can be because I know where I've come from.

Ensuring that PASS leaders support their mentees in achieving their goals, leaders transmit information and strategies that supported them through the gateway courses to a younger STEM student. In other words, PASS leaders can demonstrate what it takes to be successful in the class by addressing the uncertainty of rules and norms that can stifle students' perception of their own accomplishments early on in their college career. Taylor, a senior studying physics, provides advice to younger students and demonstrates the value of promoting close ties among students:

> And now that I'm doing the research, I'm seeing the importance in it, and I think that when I speak to my peers, and especially when I'm talking to the different freshmen in my mentor classes, I'm expressing the importance to them of getting internships and getting research opportunities, because I'm able to network. So, my major has brought me a lot of networking experience, a lot of research, and a lot of opening experiences to fields that I never had interest in, and

> it's able to get me to communicate with my peers and let
> them know how to build a relationship with your professors
> so that you can be experienced and so you can network with
> people.

Taylor is emphasizing the importance of experiences outside of the classroom. Co-curricular activities, such as research and internships, play an important role in a student's pathway to a STEM degree, oftentimes helping students translate their degrees into full-time employment or admissions into graduate programs. And in fact, the ability to "network" improves how students secure opportunities that allow them to learn about the different facets of STEM.[8] By identifying these experiences and drawing links between them, Taylor is shedding light on a path few students recognize and understand.

The benefits to this structure are also bidirectional. The cyclical nature of the Dillard programs offers students who become PASS leaders opportunities to develop their own confidence—the chance to lead, to share their story, and to motivate those coming after them. Carrie, a physics major in her junior year, shared her experience of mentoring younger students interested in pursuing physics as their major:

> I told them, "Whatever you do, this [Dillard University] is
> where it's at, like, you need to want to get it." . . . I was trying
> to get them engaged because they were like, "Oh, this is going
> to be hard," oh like they were having doubts. I'm like, "No,
> I'm doing this, this is awesome, like you can do this too."

Carrie is suggesting to her mentees that if they want to succeed in physics, they have to "want to get it." It is the will and desire to achieve that will help students overcome the difficulties—the long hours committed to studying and preparing—in STEM. Moreover, she does not deny these difficulties or how "this is going to be hard," but she does not consider them as roadblocks for the person who has a can-do attitude. The opportunity to share one's story of struggle and achievement, in turn, reveals the confidence these older students cultivate.

For Dillard University, the underrepresentation of Black students in STEM has little to do with student aspiration or ability and more to do with how institutions have failed to better help students meet the expectations and academic demands of the STEM fields. Through the PASS program, freshmen and sophomores enrolled in the gateway courses are linked with junior and senior mentors, or PASS leaders, who have successfully navigated their degree pathway. Experienced senior students can help younger students improve their performance in the gateway classes by showing that they believe in them and giving them guidance on how to walk their STEM path. The popular idiom "Seeing is believing" undergirds this Dillard practice. When someone so close to a student in age and experience is succeeding in an area they are unsure they can thrive in, working with that older student can alter their perception of themselves—that they belong and are capable of navigating, learning, and succeeding.

Perseverance through Collaboration

Common across the institutions we visited was programming that cultivated an environment in which students struggled, learned, and achieved together. By doing so, students moved on academically stronger and with an understanding that achievement is possible when the work is done in community with others. PACE (Pre-Freshman Accelerated Curriculum in Engineering) is a four-week intensive summer residential program at Morgan State University aimed at reinforcing fundamental mastery in mathematics and the sciences. While attrition remains high in the first two years of college for STEM majors, the collaborative-oriented PACE program aims to give its students an advantage so that they do not fall prey to the risk factors that commonly discourage students from completing their degrees.[9] The PACE program is intentionally difficult and was created to expand a student's capacity to manage and overcome barriers to achievement in STEM by drawing upon the encouragement and support of peers and faculty members.

What stands out the most about the PACE program is its emphasis on structure. When the associate dean of the school of engineering, Dennis Mack, arrived at Morgan State, he noticed that students' performance in class was not matching up to their intellect and high aspirations. When students arrived on campus, he explained, "There was a lot of stuff that they needed to have under their belts to even attack the [gateway] courses, because [they're] getting ready to make this big transition from high school and most of them didn't have a whole lot of structure." In addition to a rotation of courses, including English, precalculus, chemistry, biology, and computer science, and research activities to build working relationships with faculty members, students' daily schedules were structured such that their time was completely accounted for, similar to a "boot camp." Students typically woke up early, sometimes as early as 6 A.M., to complete physical training and have breakfast before attending their first class. Early in the program, students were penalized for "being late, [or] for falling asleep," but eventually students began to adjust to the regimented schedule. Their achievement was attributed to their progress in acquiring the skills to master the course material and navigate the rigors of science. Mack expanded on this:

> It's the environment from which they come. If the environment, in their high school and middle school, meaning if that structure is not there, you might have kids that have no clue as to what studying is . . . the process that you have to go through when transitioning from a high school level to a college level and the decisions that you have to make to make these things occur. I believe in [PACE] . . . what we're doing a lot of is giving them the skill sets of understanding that if you're taking a three-credit course, this is the amount of time that it's going to require for you to put into that course to pass it. It's not working harder; it's working smarter. Just teaching them those types of skill sets to understand that this is what it's going to take to survive in a STEM curriculum.

Mack draws upon the fact that many of his students graduated from K–12 systems that did provide them with the study skills to successfully undertake studies in STEM. Students can be successful if they embrace routine and structure that accommodate the amount of time and effort needed to study. The desire to succeed exists among his students, but the issue lies more in how students walk their path, either "working harder" or "working smarter." In meeting with students, we found that "working smarter" included seeing their community of peers as a strength in their learning, sense of belonging and, most importantly, capacity to persist.

"[PACE] was the worst. It was a nightmare," shared Eli, a freshman. The program was hard for a lot of students. They complained about how hard they had to work, how late they had to stay up, and how they gave up their summer, where they "didn't see the sun unless it was through the window." But no matter how harshly they described the program, not a single student regretted attending the program; in fact, looking back, they were glad. An intense four weeks with forty-nine other students imparted several benefits, one of which was cultivating social ties among peers. The common saying "The whole is greater than the sum of its parts" captures the essence of learning in engineering. Working in groups cultivated the mentality that no one individual can succeed on their own. Because the students had disparate backgrounds in preparation and exposure to math and science, working together created a pool of resources for any student to draw upon for their own learning. Maya, a freshman studying engineering, provided clarity:

> See, the thing is, even though we're saying all this bad stuff, the good part we got from it is that you learned how to work as a group, because they taught us since we're engineers we have to rely on each other. We definitely relied on each other with the homework, with the math, with the tutoring, and all the other stuff.

Similar to students at Prairie View A&M, achievement in STEM at Morgan State is not measured by how well students can perform on their own, but how well they can perform while working with others. Some students will know more than others—differences do not lead to division, but to community, where they are given greater exposure to each other's "personal lives." Take Randy, for instance. He shared with us how, in the midst of the program, he had to leave for a few days to attend a family funeral. Stressed by both the loss of a family member and the amount of work that he would need to make up, he was worried that these days off might jeopardize his progress in the program, knowing that each class provided a foundation for subsequent courses in engineering. Randy came to realize that they "had his back," which came from the slew of "calls and text messages saying, 'we wish you well'" during his time away and the hugs, care, and offers of personal tutoring he received when he returned. Establishing a community of peers before the start of the academic term can help with the transition to college because it assures the student of support in the face of challenge and difficulty both in class and in daily life. For Maya, finding friends and colleagues to study with can be difficult because of difference in goals or values, as well as a matter of comfort: "Can you be comfortable enough with them? Are they comfortable with you? Since we came through PACE, we already have that group. It just made the transition easier." The program then is structured to help students through that process of finding those with similar goals and orientations so that they start their first year with a resource of colleagues on whom they can depend when confronted with challenges in the class. "I wouldn't be able to get through my first semester if I hadn't gone through PACE and if I didn't have the people that I went through PACE with," shared Justin, a freshman.

Dennis Mack created this program to give his new students a taste of what it takes to manage and succeed in the school of engineering. With around-the-clock classes and research activities, accompanied with daily quizzes and weekly exams, students were constantly "grinding." Having a sense of the amount of time and energy needed to achieve in STEM is in part, according to Mack, a significant component in how students mentally overcome the persistent challenges that hold them accountable for their learning. Despite how terrible they felt about the PACE program earlier on, both Maya and Justin are "glad" that they went through it. Said Maya, "Now I can stay up 'til 2:00 in the morning, get my work done, or I'm able to do a lot of work in a short amount of time." Knowing one's capacity can fuel a student's sense of their own ability to persevere and achieve. At Morgan State, faculty members and staff believe that students have it in them to succeed, but that they need experiences that encourage them to learn from their peers to realize the extent of their durability and resilience in the face of challenge.

Lessons Learned

In higher education, we primarily see the student as just that: the student. They are here to absorb information and learn, and we either ignore or forget that students themselves have much to offer in how learning and achievement in STEM can be improved. Exemplified by Xavier University of Louisiana, Prairie View A&M University, Dillard University, and Morgan State University, peer-to-peer collaboration and support remain vital to these institutions' ability to address the challenges that students in STEM face.

First, we suggest that faculty members teach students early on to depend on each other. This approach pushes against the common belief that personal achievement in college is a path to walk alone.[10] Structuring curriculum and learning around the notion of cooperation— that knowledge and answers come not only from textbooks but also from one's interactions with others—is essential to building the capacity students require to overcome barriers along their trajectory in STEM. Achievement and success are almost always associated with affluent White students, but we forget that for most of them their status is an outcome of *continued support* from their parents, teachers, and friends—a fact that is hidden by the popular belief of meritocracy. Practices that privilege "personal" achievement in class and across campus only reinforce a false narrative of the world to students.

Second, encouraging students to form study groups with those who have similar goals (e.g., same major, goal of medical school) can be vital to success. Students may come from a variety of academic backgrounds, including those who did not receive strong preparation in math and science. Bringing students together opens the possibility of learning from each other and the opportunity for more advanced students to teach others, reinforcing their own knowledge of the subject matter. Building close social ties with those who share one's goals should also be framed as a solution to cultivating the capacity for increased difficulty in classes and in life. More importantly, the closeness that comes from having similar goals pours over into their social lives as well, where both learning and socializing work in tandem to create a community in which students hold each other accountable for their learning, development, and achievements.

Third, we suggest the promotion of cross-academic class interactions and relationships. Freshmen or transfer students experience moments of shock in a new academic climate, where expectations, policies and social norms can be drastically different from those of their prior schools. No students wish to fail, but few also realize that the road to success requires new and perhaps unfamiliar strategies. Studying, alone, is not sufficient for achievement. Securing full-time employment, internships, or research opportunities requires knowing how to build and capitalize on academic and professional relationships. For instance, cultivating a meaningful relationship through research with faculty members, who can lend legitimacy to a student's expressed interest in an opportunity, is a bridge that can help the student travel from their education and degree to future success. Older students can share these practices and hidden rules of engagement early in the first year of new students, priming them to maximize the benefits of higher education.

In an era when colleges and universities are asking faculty members to teach more, conduct more research, and provide more service, they might have little time left to support students academically and professionally. Creating programs that invite students to be a part of a peer-to-peer mentoring and tutoring network addresses the strain on faculty members while still mitigating the inequality—derived from students' unequal academic and social experiences prior to college—witnessed in college. Cooperation and community rather than personal competition are how students at these HBCUs thrive in competitive fields in STEM. Conditioning students to normalize "support" and "community" in STEM is part of the larger messages of inclusivity that students receive on their campuses.

4

Messages and Examples
of Inherent Inclusivity

COLLEGES AND UNIVERSITIES ARE OFTEN rewarded for being exclusive. Being competitive, climbing in the rankings, weeding people out of academic programs and fighting over the "best" students is the norm on many college and university campuses. In contrast, most HBCUs focus on being inclusive—some even have an open enrollment policy—based on an inherent belief that all students can be successful.[1]

Many predominantly white institutions (PWIs) give Black students the message that academic success is not in their future.[2] This is how racism works, conceiving of an individual's potential based on the color of their skin or their cultural background. Racism excludes Black students from opportunities and spaces that many perceive as being beyond their intellect and capabilities—opportunities and spaces on which the majority places a premium, such as STEM fields. Racism causes psychological harm to Black students, and in a culture of higher education that thrives on exclusivity as the definitive measure of success, sends a message that only a few can pursue and succeed in STEM or STEM-related occupations. At the HBCUs in our study, a belief in students' ability to be successful was defined by a barrage of messages expressing inclusivity—nothing but the student's own desires could or should hold a student back.

An institutional or departmental culture with a history of championing achievement can help African American students embrace and translate their own aspirations into earning a STEM degree. For African American students, encountering a culture of success can serve as a form of momentum to springboard them to success of their own. All too often faculty members in STEM at PWIs may think that they assume success and foster success for all students, but the experiences of African Americans tell us the opposite story.[3] Students often feel ignored, discounted, and unable to form close relationships with STEM faculty members. Assuming inherent success and seeing African American students as capable of success from day one of their STEM experience can make a fundamental difference in how they perceive the likelihood and trajectory of their achievement. In this chapter, we report some of the messages that faculty members share with students to engender their success and the voices of students as they navigate a challenging academic terrain steeped in a deep and inclusive belief in their potential. We also provide guidance to institutions that lack a history of success for African Americans or that have failed to champion success, helping them to capitalize on small and intermediate accomplishments as they move forward with a new commitment to more fully supporting underrepresented students.

Capitalizing on a History of Successes

HBCUs have an extensive history of graduating successful African American leaders, educators, and innovators, a legacy that should be celebrated and heralded.[4] Capitalizing on past successes of African Americans provides a high degree of momentum for students, especially for students coming from environments where Black success is rarely recognized or celebrated.[5]

HBCUs' legacy in STEM provides a foundation of success and inclusivity on which current colleges and universities can build. HBCU students regularly see highly successful individuals associated with the institutions and in front of them in the classroom. In contrast to PWIs, HBCUs have a rich legacy of graduating African Americans in science. This history and track record of success is often championed in their classrooms. All too often, as we have seen, science and science training are centered on Whites and men, normalizing their leadership and pervasive presence in the field. HBCUs disrupt this roadblock to Black students' success, both by their very existence and by centering African American success. Not only do HBCUs build on the successes of their famous STEM alumni—such as surgeon and researcher Charles Drew, botanist George Washington Carver, physician and former U.S. surgeon general Regina Benjamin, and physician and former U.S. secretary of health and human services Louis W. Sullivan—they build upon the great numbers of everyday alumni who are working as professors, doctors, nurses, pharmacists, and researchers across the nation.[6]

Colleges and universities are in the business of recruiting, educating, and graduating students. A powerful way to draw students in and engage and empower them is to promote the school's history of achievement. Woven into and glorified in these narratives are famous writers and poets, famed scientists and their discoveries, and alumni who are leaders of industry. Overwhelmingly, the PWI narratives whitewash the past, ignore and dismiss histories of slavery and racism, and ignore the achievements of racial minorities and women.[7] One of the most powerful aspects of HBCUs is the way they capitalize on their rich histories and legacies.

When a student shares that she wants to become a medical professional, the response is almost always one of admiration and inspiration because medicine is considered a difficult and exclusive path.[8] Only 4 percent of those who have successfully walked this path are Black.[9] Racially, the odds of admission into medical school are stacked against them. A message of racial exclusion is not lost on students in our research. In fact, it drives them to choose an HBCU for their premed education because at HBCUs histories of Black achievement are celebrated and messages of inclusion and success are commonplace—Black students' aspirations and presence in premedical courses are not questioned, but embraced and cultivated.

The hallways of Xavier University of Louisiana are lined with photos of their alumni and past institutional leaders, Black individuals who have overcome barriers to opportunity and achievement. These images remind students of a past in which Black educational opportunity for higher learning was limited to HBCUs. However, they are also proof of a student's own resilience and potential to achieve in an era in which racial discrimination and overt prejudices are illegal and considered morally wrong, but nonetheless continue to persist and affect students in pernicious ways.

Xavier University of Louisiana has a formidable and famous history of producing doctors, which can be credited to Norman Francis, the school's long-serving president.[10] In the 1970s Francis read a report that caused him great concern—the report sounded the alarm that the number of Black doctors in the U.S. was dwindling at a steady pace.

Francis was a man of action and decided to focus on becoming a major producer of Blacks in STEM and, more specifically, Black doctors. As a result of consistent efforts over many decades, Xavier University produces more Black graduates who apply to and graduate from medical school than any other college or university in the country.[11]

From students' points of view, attending Xavier gives them the confidence that they will succeed in becoming a doctor. They have few doubts about the future they wish to achieve. Xavier's track record is well known among prospective students and is communicated with large billboards around the campus and throughout the surrounding states. African American communities know of Xavier's record of success in medicine. Of its nearly 3,000 undergraduates in any year, 20 percent are pursuing degrees in chemistry, a subject critical for admission to medical and other health professional schools.[12] Students know that success has come before them and that they will demonstrate success for those in the future. Felecia, a sophomore, shared her reasons for coming to Xavier: "I came to Xavier because I had a cousin who came, and then she told me how good they were with science programs, and that they were geared towards getting people into medical school. I just felt like for me it was the best option to get myself into medical school."

Students understand the history of Xavier and how this history will propel them to individual success. Another student, Dafina, explained it to us in this way:

> One of the main driving points for me coming to Xavier was their success rate. Every time Xavier was mentioned, every time I say I go to Xavier University in Louisiana, people say, "Oh, you want to become a doctor!" because they just know that Xavier University breeds doctors, successful doctors, all

over the country. We are successful in every aspect, and every region, all over the world. Every time I'm studying, I say okay, it's been done before, I can do this, and I just have to keep going.

Xavier's reputation is profound, but Xavier is not unique in graduating large numbers of students who go on to be successful doctors. The difference is that Xavier enrolls ample numbers of African Americans—the institution bets on the potential success of these students, whereas other schools are not willing to take the same risks. Xavier's first-year students have an average GPA of 3.37 and an average SAT combined math and verbal score of 985, and 57 percent of the school's first-year students are Pell Grant recipients. According to the Association of American Medical Colleges, "medical school matriculants often come from middle and upper income families," whereas a little over a third of Black medical students come working class homes.[13] In light of this national context, the odds are stacked against Black students seeking a career in medicine. And yet, Xavier has fewer resources than PWIs but takes the risk and succeeds in a way that fosters future success and hope in the minds of African Americans.

The supportive environment at Xavier University came from the top. President Norman Francis communicated the belief in every student's success to each student from the moment they stepped on campus. Students told us that during orientation, the president communicated a message of success that ran counter to what their friends at other institutions heard: "President Francis spoke. And he said, 'You know how most schools will say only 85 percent of you guys will graduate, everybody that you're sitting next to won't graduate?' He said, 'No, we don't say that here, everybody will graduate at the end of the four years.' So it's like you don't have a choice." From the time they step onto campus, students are constantly reminded of everyone's potential to succeed. This message of success, however, is framed around inclusiveness—a significant contrast to PWIs' messages that Black students don't belong in the college pipeline.[14]

Like Xavier University, Prairie View A&M University has a deep history of fostering success in medicine. Generations of their students have become doctors. One of the institution's approaches to ensuring that students see themselves as successful is to bring former students—now successful alumni serving as doctors across the nation—back to campus at the beginning of the academic year and throughout students' academic programs. Bernard, a student at Prairie View A&M, told us that his professor ensures that students see success regularly and prominently,

> He brings in people like doctors, dentists, veterinarians that are already making it and doing what we want to do. He brings them in and they motivate us, tell us what we need to do, and they help us along. They're also African American, so it helps, as some people don't have that mindset that they can do whatever they want to do.

Perhaps Prairie View biology professor Lynette Shaw says it best: "When you have a person who graduated from Prairie View and they come back and they tell you their journey, it makes a difference, and you can see that they are successful—the PhDs, the physicians, the dentists, the pharmacist, the podiatrist, the physical therapist, occupational therapist." One of the Prairie View students, Jackie, enthusiastically affirmed Shaw's assertion:

> I've been in the situation where I was the only Black woman. So sometimes it's harder because some students may not un-

derstand you as well, as far as your background, or they may not be as receptive to listening to you and things that you have to say. So it does help. When you see people like you pushing forward through the certain struggles that they have to go through, it pushes you to push even harder because you look at them and you're like, okay, you're going through this right now, so I know I can push even harder because I'm not even in that situation.

Seeing demonstrated success not only matters to students when they are in school but serves as an impetus for future and sustained success. It offers a glimpse into their own possibilities as well as their capacity to push forward.

Faculty members and faculty buy-in around promoting success are essential to student success because faculty control the curriculum and day-to-day student interactions in STEM classes. The biology department at Prairie View A&M University has a pedigree of success. Families of students have attended the institution. Students often know before coming to the institution that they will be supported, uplifted, and believed in. They know because their cousins, parents, sisters, and brothers have attended the school and are a demonstration and manifestation of the success that is possible. Zoe, a student, explained this idea to us with a sense of security in her mother's point of view and how it inspired her,

I chose Prairie View because my mom told me, I was looking at other schools. [An elite, southern, private university] was my first choice, and I had all other schools that I was looking at, like bigger schools with more recognition, like whenever you heard the name. But my mom told me,

"If you want to become a doctor, you need to go to Prairie View. Prairie View is where people go to become doctors." That's why I decided to come to Prairie View.

Most colleges and universities have a record of success in STEM but fail to realize how important it is for that record to include racial and ethnic diversity. All too often, those leading premedical programs define success without attention to diversity, not realizing the long-term, negative impact this has on African American students' perceptions of belonging in a space that is dominated by White doctors. Even when established STEM programs achieve success among African Americans, they often fail to highlight this success or to keep in touch with graduates.

Believing in Success Even When Students Might Not

An institutional culture of success surrounds students with messages of success and empowerment. These include messages that come from the president, the faculty members, and the student support staff, who need to have a belief in students that is more profound than the beliefs students have in themselves—because feeling sure of having support is essential for students, especially for students who may not have received that quality of support from prior teachers. Thomas Owens, a Prairie View A&M University biology professor, exemplifies the idea of believing deeply in student success:

A student came in to see me after his high school teachers (the math teacher and the chemistry teacher) told him to. They said, "You need to go talk to Dr. Owens. We don't think you're going to make it. We don't think you can be a doctor."

Tears were coming out of his eyes. I said, "You can do it. You can be a medical doctor—but only if you're going to close that gap." I said, "While other students are asleep, you will need to be studying. You've got to study every day, including Sunday, and you've got to catch up." What do you think he did? He did exactly that. I would come in on Sundays and Saturdays, and he was always in there studying. Even during the day between classes, he'd be in my research lab studying. So today—oh, by the way, he caught them. He passed them up. He caught his cohort, and he passed them up. So at the end of the third year, he was the first one accepted to Texas A&M University Medical School.

Owens stressed that he often believes in the capabilities and potential success of students more than they do themselves, because this is necessary when the messages students bring into college are damaging their confidence and limiting their view of their future. David, one of his students, confirmed Professor Owens's commitment:

He wants us to believe in ourselves, and he also wants us to be confident. I remember when I was drawing a molecule for the class, and he asked me if I thought that it was right. I was like, "Probably not." He said, "No, it is. But I want you to know that it's right." He taught me that I need to be more confident with what I answer or whenever I'm taking a test, anything in general. I have to believe in myself and my abilities.

The care and attention demonstrated by Owens is life-changing for students because it pushes against a dominant false societal narrative of Black inferiority in STEM and the medical profession.

At Dillard University in New Orleans, the school culture of success is spearheaded by its president, Walter Kimbrough, who is dedicated to the superior performance of his students and ensuring their success despite the odds against them. Kimbrough came to the presidency from a nontraditional path—as a vice president of student affairs—which gives him a special inclination toward students, about which he is quite vocal. Students know that their success is the centerpiece at Dillard and other HBCUs. Gina, a student at Dillard, told us:

> I would basically say at an HBCU, I feel like there are stronger values and morals around Black success. So, when African Americans come to these institutions, the main goal is to get you out successfully. You're not competing with anybody. We're not in a competition. It's just to make sure that you're here and we're going to teach you what you need to know so that you can compete with any race or ethnicity that you're put in the room with at any given time for any different career.

When students understand that their success is paramount to an institution, they feel empowered to succeed. Prairie View A&M University biology professor Bill Porter reported:

> I'm going to do whatever it takes to get the students to reach the bar and cross the bar, and I'm not going to lower the bar. I tell my students, "Hey, an A in my class, an A student in my class, should be an A student at Harvard or any other majority institution." So, I mean, I think the culture now is: we have to dig deep to unleash the greatness into our students. If that means working hard with them one on one, changing

the way you develop your teaching strategies, do what it has to take.

Porter believes in students even when they might doubt themselves:

> These kids have got so much promise in them—they do—so much potential. But you've got to tap into it. And if you don't tap into it, they don't even know it's there. You've got to let them know, "Hey, you know what, you might have been a C+ student in high school, but you know what? There's greatness inside of you." That's what I think a lot of the faculty members do here. We can acknowledge or see a potential in our students, and we'll pull it out and give them confidence. Once they know they can do it, they're on fire and they take off.

Porter seeks students out and pushes them to be at the level of success he believes they have the unlimited potential to achieve. When we talked with him, he was smiling and excited about working with students:

> I seek them out. I seek them out. I seek them out because a lot of our students, a lot of the guys . . . our ratio for students is two-thirds women and the rest are men. I tell the guys right off the bat—I say, "Look, I'm going to call on you every day in class. No guy is going to sit up in class and not participate." So I call on them. So I let them know that I'm going to stay in their face. Like the guy, Eric, who's in my class now, he used to be in my anatomy and physiology class. He would sit back. I would ask him a question, and he goes, "Oh,

Dr. Porter, I don't know." I said, "Do you think that's cool, to say you don't know?" I said, "You know what, we're going to sit here until you answer the question." The whole class will sit there like, "Dude, would you say something!" And then finally he started participating. I let him know.

Often hearing his students joking with and yelling at each in the hallways, Porter encourages students to use their voices in the classroom by noting their ample ability to use them outside of the classroom. He challenges students to bring all their confidence and words from the hallways into his classes, and presents learning as a way to demonstrate their strengths. One of his students shared with us Porter's message, telling us, "When classes would get tough, because they do get tough, he would always be like, 'You can do it. You can do it. Believe in yourself.'" Students notice and appreciate his confidence in them.

At Xavier University of Louisiana students face a grueling curriculum that challenges them night and day. At the same time, they have access to teachers who champion their success. Students are encouraged to believe in themselves but are provided a safety net when the semester gets rough—a safety net that many first-generation and low-income students otherwise would not have. According to Ana, that safety net is the support of the faculty members who push her even when she is unsure of her own abilities and stamina for finishing, "Simply because of people who have been with me and that have pushed me, even when I was unsure of myself, they made sure I knew that, 'You're fully capable of doing that.'"

Black colleges in this study define success widely for students.[15] When students do not achieve A's in their classes, they are not dismissed as not being good enough to pursue PhDs and MDs. Instead they are counseled, pushed, and inspired by their faculty members. Their teachers work with them to create a roadmap for achieving higher performance in classes, rather than assuming students do not have the intellect or ability to conquer the coursework. Xavier University student Patrice told us, "I wasn't supposed to be a tutor, because I got a B in organic chemistry for my second semester. But I guess my professor saw something in me that I didn't see, and she [said], 'No, you don't have to have A's in both chemistries, you can still do it if you have a B in one of them.'"

What would happen if STEM faculty members at colleges and universities across the country took their focus off the highest-achieving students and placed more focus on those students at the next level, who are striving but need more support, advising, and input? Unfortunately, many faculty members tie their own worth to the success of their students, preferring to work with only the "top students"—many of whom are White and come from middle- to upper-class homes—and pay little attention to those students who need more work and are striving, or in some cases struggling, to succeed.[16] Narrow definitions of promise and success not only exclude students from opportunities, they also operate to widen gaps in racial achievement.[17]

Nydia Douglas, a chemistry professor at Xavier University, revealed that the faculty members believe in the potential of all their students: "We encourage them to go. When they come to us unprepared, we make sure to give them the best we can to prepare them. When they come to us prepared, we try to provide them with opportunities to excel in what they're doing, to put them in programs that put them in the lab, provide them with experience." Faculty members explained to us that students are fully aware that their teachers want them to be successful and that not being successful is not an option. Faculty expectations are high: "The students really know that we are watching them carefully and that we are invested in their success, so they don't have an excuse. They can't come up with an excuse." Students understand the commitment of the institution and their department faculty members and use the commitment as a source of motivation. Felecia, a student at Xavier, puts it this way:

> It's set up so you're not going to fail. If you're struggling, there are so many resources. Professors will come to you and they will talk to you. Professors will email me, asking, "How are you doing? What should I change? Any suggestions?" They're very open and willing to help. They want to see you succeed. It's not like you're left to your own devices to learn everything and understand the material.

Faculty are proactive with students. Student success is prioritized in the design and delivery of curricula so that faculty members can coordinate with each other to anticipate student needs.

Lessons from HBCUs' Commitment to Success

As the nation continues to ask questions about how to engender success among African American students in STEM, the answers are right in front of us and are rooted in a long history that begins with a belief in inclusive success. There is much to learn from HBCUs about cultivating a culture of success for African Americans across all colleges and universities and for students more broadly. Although the environment and culture of HBCUs cannot be replicated at other schools, the commitment to the success of students can be embraced. Predominantly

White institutions can start by seeing all students as having value and by understanding the school's role in students' success.[18]

First, as with all priorities in the college and university context, a dedication to the success of African Americans in STEM must come from the top. Success must be at the forefront of the school president's communications with faculty members and support staff. Leaders often speak about rigor and selectivity, not realizing that it would be more empowering, and would lead to wider success, to instead speak about inclusivity and how the institution can benefit students and support them. Bragging about who does not get admitted to an institution and boasting about selectivity only promotes competition, which can push out students who are unable to meet the school's narrow metrics of achievement—which are based on narrow notions of college readiness and can make the less-prepared students feel unqualified to pursue a degree in STEM. Imagine if more institutions made an effort to identify the learning gaps that many African American students may have—based on their lack of access to a high-quality K–12 education, and not on their ability—and closed those gaps by creating environments that communicate inclusiveness and pathways to success for African American students. There is an enormous need for more STEM-educated graduates in the United States, and our colleges and universities could fill that need by promoting inclusivity and success for all students—placing students at the heart of schooling.

Second, the faculty members at the ten HBCUs in this study demonstrate the impact of emphasizing African American student success from the time students step foot on campus and throughout their time in the classroom. Depending on one's background and family access to a college education, a belief in oneself can be difficult to develop. Often the push or support of a faculty member against negative narratives that many Black students have internalized is what makes the difference between failure and accomplishment. Even African Americans who hail from middle-class, well-educated families face daily microaggressions that challenge their mere presence on college campuses.

HBCU faculty members teach us that success does not mean perfection and that students who are not earning all A's still have potential in STEM. Their dips in achievement may be due to outside forces in their lives, lack of opportunity, and the teaching style of their professors. When African American students are not doing well in STEM classes, we must ask ourselves why and figure out what we are failing to do or provide. We need to understand that the B students might have achieved immensely in classes, given their backgrounds, and that this kind of success must also be cultivated and celebrated. Moreover, we need to realize that opportunities for success must be shared in equitable ways—not equal, but equitable, making up for past injustice. These HBCUs understand that not all their students enter with the same background and that therefore success must be measured in light of their personal circumstances.

5

Students' Needs over Faculty Members' Needs

INCREASED DEMANDS FOR FACULTY MEMBERS to produce more research and take on more administrative responsibilities can often take away their focus on students' needs and desires to learn.[1] From the moment students enter PhD programs at research universities, they are taught to craft their own research agenda, that single-authored work is more valuable, and that teaching should be approached in an efficient and expedient manner.[2] Doctoral students are rarely encouraged to collaborate and instead often see their peers as competition. As these students graduate and move into faculty positions, they employ the same approach they learned in graduate school and begin to mentor their students in similar ways. Rather than focusing on conducting meaningful research with a cadre of the best minds, or teaching students with the support of their peers, faculty members typically venture off on their own, knowing that their work as an individual will be rewarded more fully by a tenure system that fetishizes the lone researcher—or, in many STEM fields, the principal investigator of the lab, who rarely speaks of teaching or considers deviating from traditional models of learning.[3] And faculty members who don't work alone will often demand the lead role in research because this position is the most prestigious.

The idea of the lone researcher plays out in various ways in research, but the manner in which it manifests in teaching is particularly dangerous if students thrive instead under a more community-oriented classroom environment.[4] The typical approach to teaching is for faculty members to develop their own classes, with their own syllabus, and then teach the class in a vacuum—the course is shaped without consultation with other faculty members and without considering the content of other courses. Rarely do faculty members ask for input on their syllabi or teaching. Courses and syllabi are approved routinely, and courses are rarely reviewed afterward except when an institution is undergoing accreditation. At many major research institutions, faculty members are given the option of teaching what they want to teach, plus an occasional required course. They rarely convene with other faculty members to talk about their classes or, more importantly, how their classes speak to student needs, learning outcomes, and other courses in the major. There is immense freedom at many institutions when it comes to teaching, and this freedom is what draws many graduates to choose teaching. The demands of the academy and the tenure-award structure, however, can make it difficult for faculty to develop and maintain effective learning environments for their students. Our research at the ten HBCUs tells us how faculty members can overcome those demands to support their students.[5]

At the HBCUs we visited, faculty members in the STEM fields worked together to craft STEM curricula that were designed to validate the background of students and, ultimately, amplify their learning. Often this approach meant hiring new people with a team-based outlook or spending countless hours ensuring that all classes complemented one another. This approach challenges conventional notions of teaching and disrupts the nearly cemented status quo in STEM curricula. Faculty members who are compelled to learn what others are doing in their classes, and who build on the contributions of their colleagues, are more able to ensure long-term student learning and success. Moreover, institutions that are committed to student learning reward innovative and collaborative approaches to teaching in their tenure and promotion processes.

The HBCU Approach

The HBCU faculty members in the STEM fields whom we interviewed worked together to craft STEM curricula designed to validate students' varied backgrounds as a way to amplify students' learning. To foster this kind of environment, the faculty members create an ethos of teamwork over individuality. Faculty members are friends, eat lunch together, socialize together, talk about how to support students as a group, and offer support to each other as they grapple with finding new and innovative ways to teach. We are not saying that these faculties operate in perfect harmony—no faculty does—but they were committed to meeting, talking, debating, growing, and centering student learning. The HBCUs we visited looked to hire new faculty members who were willing to focus on working in teams and sharing ideas across the curriculum. Their "weeding out" involved not hiring applicants who seemed to prioritize themselves over the needs of students. Still other HBCUs worked to disrupt what is commonly learned in graduate school from mentors, demonstrating that working as a team in service to the students is more effective than working solo. These HBCUs approached student success by valuing coordination and connectedness among faculty members in order to create a learning experience that acknowledges the diverse ways that students can effectively learn.

At Xavier University, members of the chemistry faculty use a common syllabus to make it easier for students to understand the curricula. The syllabus brings together assignments, office hours, and a "drill" system for ensuring that students understand the material. Students are encouraged to go to any of the faculty members teaching the course across the department, which is usually about six or seven. Sometimes students assume that they should go to the same faculty member for class, drills, and office hours, but one faculty member told us that students are encouraged to go to different faculty members because they might understand a concept better when having it explained by another faculty member. Rather than engender an academic community that maintains that one professor is better than another, which is typical in most academic departments, at Xavier, students are encouraged to see the nuances in the way faculty members explain concepts and to understand that these nuances could be the difference between understanding and failing to grasp a concept.

Once faculty members embrace the ethos of teamwork, they learn to build on what their colleagues are doing in classes, and this approach leads to increased student learning. At Xavier University, Linda Taylor, a professor of chemistry, told us,

> For general chemistry, we have a weekly meeting, a weekly lecture meeting where we just talk about what's going on in

the class, and . . . we are constantly revising this and . . . talking about how we covered concepts. And if somebody says, "Oh, I did this and it worked in my class," and everybody's an author on this, . . . it's built into the ownership.

Wanda Lawson, another Xavier professor of chemistry, described working together with faculty members in this way:

> The flipside is, since we have so many faculty members, it is coordinated. So we tell people up front, "If you teach one of these coordinated classes, everyone has input, we meet regularly." There's a policy, everyone votes on it, and that's what you follow the next year. If it doesn't work, we revisit that policy. But to make a good product for the student, we all teach out of the same book, we all follow the same schedule.

Not only does the Xavier approach lead to a more student-centered learning environment, it serves as a foundation for a healthy community for faculty members and to a collaborative, instead of competitive, working environment. Many PWIs are structured to privilege faculty members' research above all else, encouraging faculty members to make decisions that minimize their commitment to teaching. Under these conditions, it can become very difficult to get faculty members to coordinate and share resources with each other and be available to students that they do not know.

HBCU professors often organize classes around their own knowledge and expertise and students' specific level of knowledge acquisition. Sally Ware, another faculty member at Xavier University, told us that you must teach where the students are—at their level of preparation—or you will lose them. She recommended giving students streamlined and organized information and ensuring that they know what information is most important: "Sometimes they write down everything coming out of your mouth and don't know what is really important." To bolster students' performance throughout the chemistry program at Xavier, the faculty members have used a common textbook that focuses on drills, which are held several times a week. The textbook, which is ever changing and added to regularly, is the brainchild of J. W. Carmichael. It is published and sold in the bookstore, and ensures that students master the fundamentals of chemistry that are key to subsequent courses in their majors. Carmichael was a professor at Xavier University most of his life and firmly believed in doing everything possible to ensure students' success. When asked what his greatest accomplishment was, he replied, "As far as I am concerned, the only accomplishment worthwhile was being able to look back at any time and say that I had done everything humanly possible to help as many students achieve their goal of becoming a health professional."[6] Carmichael's legacy permeates the textbook because it established an environment in which every faculty member knows what is being taught across the curriculum and in which students are focused on learning chemistry—how its fundamental principles are connected—rather than on what to write down and memorize. For faculty to prioritize students' needs over their own means adopting this text and its procedures, even if it may go against the dominant norms of the academy.

Often when Xavier University faculty members explain their teaching and learning process to faculty from other universities, these non-HBCU faculty see the Xavier approach as "hand-holding." But that's not the way Xavier faculty see it. They see the results, which include students who perform well on national placement and licensure tests, remember concepts a full two years later, and achieve their goals of becoming faculty members, doctors, and pharmacists. "Part of the design of the classes is that we make students do drills, we make them do homework and study every week, even though they don't have a test. We are showing them that to be successful, you can't study once a month, you have to study every day." The design of this approach goes well beyond weekly preparations for lectures. It requires faculty members to anticipate student needs in every facet of their learning: What they take away from the initial lecture, how well they apply the information from the lecture to the weekly quizzes, and how much enlightenment they receive when they are provided with faculty feedback. The strict attention to student learning keeps students accountable for their own choices and helps them learn how to monitor their progress for the future.

Taylor, a teacher in the chemistry department at Xavier, explained that the drills are an enormous amount of work, but the payoff is significant: "It's a lot of grading. It's a lot of time. It's a lot of office hours. But I think that is probably the primary reason for our success, that we work so much with the students." Because current faculty members understand the demands of the chemistry curriculum, they share syllabi with new faculty members to ensure that they can easily come up to speed. Said Regina Fuller, a chemistry faculty member, "We have a certain kind of style, and it takes some time to get acclimated to it. . . . Yes, you have to give up a little freedom. But when you come [here], there's so much support; you can just hit the ground running, you don't need to reinvent the wheel."

The drill manual that guides faculty and students in chemistry has a checklist for students and a checklist for faculty. Each student is held accountable for the material and for learning the material in an intense and routine manner. The drill manual holds faculty accountable—"It's a system of checks and balances." Faculty have to put a significant amount of time and energy into the drill system, but the students deeply appreciate the effort—and the results are remarkable. Sally Ware described how drills work and why they are important:

> At first it is a complicated system, and we tell them that the first day. We say, "If you're going to take general chemistry anywhere else, you're probably going to go to class two or three times a week, and once in a while you'll take notes, and once in a while you'll have an exam, and that's how you take general chemistry. But this is what we do in general chemistry here at Xavier." And I understand there are a lot of pieces, so the first few weeks . . . every time I go to lecture, I say, "Okay, this is what you're going to turn in, in drill, and this is what you're going to have a quiz over." And I show them a calendar just to get them familiar, because it is complicated, and they are kind of overwhelmed at first. But, by and large, once they get into it, they like it.

She added,

> I sell this to them. I say, "We do this because we want you to stay on track." A lot of times, students wait until the night before to study for the test, and you just can't do that. And because we have weekly drills, that keeps students up to date, that keeps students current, so they don't wait until the night before the test to study. And then you make sure that you're on point when you take an exam. They are science students, and most science students like routine, they like structure.

Despite the drill manual's demand on faculty members' time, in which they must assess and provide feedback on weekly exams, it is a process that they buy into year after year.

Exams at Xavier University also work differently in chemistry. Rather than have separate tests for each class, faculty members co-create exams. Fuller explained:

> We all submit questions, and then we all get a copy of the test. We review it and get our comments back to the coordinator before we make up the test, every time. We make up a new test every year, make up a new final every year. And that's also a check-and-balance system because I have to be teaching in a way that my students can answer anybody's organic chemistry questions.

Also, of note, the faculty members build the exams so that the questions get harder as a student moves deeper into the exam. Some questions speak to C students and should be easily mastered, whereas others take the skill of an A student. Faculty members work together to create exams that keep students accountable for learning the key building blocks of chemistry and that help them monitor their students' progress. Each year, when they revisit the exams, they work to root out exam questions that are misleading or unnecessarily tricky or do not speak to the most relevant aspects of learning chemistry.

Engineering faculty at Morgan State University use a similar approach to ensure that their students learn the material. According to one professor, Barry Wilkins, "These students don't come from math-rich backgrounds, and for them to be brought up to speed and learn the foundational material for engineering, we have to give them daily quizzes. They have to be focused on the material every day." The

Morgan State faculty members insisted that, despite lacking sufficient math skills when they enter college, students can learn the material if it is practically applied and used every day. It takes a great deal of energy for these professors to create and grade daily quizzes, but they put the needs of their students above their own and realize that they must work hard to make up for the disparities that students experienced at the K–12 level.

At Delaware State University, Shirley Hart, a professor, told us that she realized that students were not entirely sure how to read a textbook, meaning that they did not know how to parse out what was most important. She spent time showing students how to read deeply and efficiently, using videos that she made herself. What we found at these HBCUs is that there is a commitment to use every tool available to ensure that students learn. Faculty members often teach developmental math to students in the summer before their first year so that they can start college-level math when the fall semester begins. Students are not overlooked due to challenges they face in math or steered away from pursuing a degree in science; instead they are helped, motivated, and cheered on by faculty and staff. To combat students' frustration in math, the faculty members spend time designing activities that involve practical and real-world examples, because research shows that students can grasp abstract concepts much more easily when they are applied in problem-based models. Moreover, they combine traditional methods of teaching science with online support, creating tools that can be used outside the classroom when students are studying on their own. Overall, the focus is on finding out where students are stumbling, revamping those areas, and creating learning environments that make it easier for them to understand the material. This type of approach does take more time, but it helps their students achieve actual and long-lasting learning.

Sally Ware explains the approach of going the extra mile for students at Xavier and her commitment to it:

> One student, who was my research student, he works for Exxon now, and got an industry job when he graduated. He struggled a lot. He was struggling in organic chemistry, and he retook the class. I said, "Let's study over the break. You come talk to me when you retake it. Bring me all your questions. We'll meet before class starts." And I tell this to all of the students who don't pass. He did it, and he got an A the second time he took it. We wrote a grant proposal and got him in the lab, and got him into research. And he worked for Exxon, and he just got promoted. The point is that you might not be successful in what it was that you thought you wanted to do when you were seventeen and started here, but if you're going to be successful at something, then let's find it.

We found that the HBCU faculty members are willing to dig deep to find the greatness in students, not giving up when students failed or faltered. They worked hard to help students identify and cultivate their passions by providing opportunities for them to realize their capacity in STEM.

It was a similar underlying idea that led the faculty at Morgan State University to create their summer boot camp to combat the lack of knowledge in math and the lack of organizational skills that many of their engineering students arrive with in their first year. Said Professor Richard Barnes, "There are a lot of things that these students need to have under their belts in order to begin classes, such as coming to class on time, having structure in their lives, and being disciplined about being an engineer." The boot camp is focused on "undergirding the academic rigor of the engineering program with structure." Students are expected to get up early in the morning, exercise, eat properly, and then participate in a rotation of precalculus, chemistry, biology, computer science, and engineering. The boot camp is vital to the students' success, but it also requires faculty to put in a significant amount of work. They must be committed to the success of students. Students have quizzes every day, and the program is intense, with a high level of human interaction. When we talked to faculty members about the program, they admitted that it took considerable work, but its success seemed to be the reward. Professor Daryl Roberts told us, "I have data to show that once you put the kids in that summer program, and then you provide the right services to them from their sophomore year to their junior year, you are fine. Then I think once that occurs, you can let them go and they do very well." Faculty members know that the extra effort on the front end pays off with students more fully understanding course material, staying in college, graduating, and acquiring positions in engineering.

One way that the engineering faculty members at Morgan State University convince new faculty recruits to invest this kind of time in students on the front end is by sharing with them longitudinal data that show the impact of the boot camp and student performance in the overall engineering program. Several faculty members regularly collect data pertaining to student performance across the engineering program—looking at peer-to-peer interaction, test performance, and class performance with various interventions. These faculty members even publish academic papers pertaining to these data and secure grant funding to conduct the research. The engineering faculty at Morgan State have connected their investment in students to research that moves the field of engineering forward and helps others to understand what works in terms of fostering success with African American students. And students see the investment that faculty members make as essential to their learning, as is the intensity of the attention they receive. In the words of Anna, a sophomore, "During that period, where they forced us to do work, I learned it, I relearned it, and I made sure that I memorized it, because there was nothing else to do because we were forced to do work. Now, since I learned the material, it makes my classes a lot easier with respect to calculus 1 and calculus 2." When students see that faculty are wholly invested in them, they often give their very best effort.

STEM faculty also must do research, which often requires reducing their course load. At North Carolina Central University, the course load is quite high, but in order to give faculty additional time for their research, other faculty will often step in and take on additional courses to teach. This occurs under the premise that everyone in the department not only will occasionally take on a higher course load, but also will occasionally have the opportunity to teach a reduced course load. David Copeland, a senior academic administrator at North Carolina Central University, explained how faculty members in these situations are supported:

> If I have a junior faculty member who's working on a re-
> search project and . . . [who is] really at that moment where
> you really need to get this done . . . then I should have the
> right to give that person a reduced teaching load. And we're
> going to carry the load for the department somehow. But let
> me give [a particular professor] a reduced load. Everybody
> gets their turn. So, you handle that even though, as you

know, we don't have an official policy of sabbatical and all of that, but there are ways to do that. And so, we have somewhat instilled that, to help faculty meet that type of research load.

Wealthier schools have the funds to hire graduate students or adjuncts to teach the additional course load, but North Carolina Central University does not have this luxury. The school depends on the willingness of faculty to pitch in and support each other so that all faculty members will have an opportunity to pursue their research. The research itself is needed in order to give students lab experiences that bridge classroom learning with real-world applications.

Labs are educational environments that promote student learning. Greater exposure to lab work is associated with improved STEM educational outcomes for minority students, so it is critical for institutions to provide the appropriate opportunities for lab work. Labs, however, require funding, which faculty must find the time to apply for and bring in. Having a reduced teaching load can help a faculty member find that time to identify and apply for funding opportunities.

Larger and more resourced schools receive much higher levels of funding than HBCUs. The cost to create a lab with basic necessities can range from $500,000 to $1 million. This kind of funding is not readily available at an HBCU. According to Kira McNeil, a professor at Xavier University:

> If you're in a smaller institution, you [have to work] with limited funds. And now we've seen a lot of success (not that we weren't successful before) . . . [due to] the research grants . . . we've received. But . . . you don't have the funds so that everyone who needs . . . some big piece of equip-

ment . . . can have one in their own labs. We must work together and prioritize. . . . The faculty work together . . . we
get this one piece of equipment . . . and then share it.

Because the capacity to apply for funding is limited by a faculty member's responsibility to teaching, working together allows faculty to successfully seek funding while maintaining faithful to the student-
centered culture. Moreover, although funds may belong to a single
faculty member, the resources purchased with the funds are shared
with all teachers in the department, which makes it easier for all faculty members to provide lab experiences for their own students. Despite a full plate of teaching, research, and administrative responsibilities, faculty members collaborating together can bring in the necessary
resources to address the needs of their students.

Talking across the Disciplines

Faculty members are inherently discipline-based.[7] Rather than having
an allegiance to their institution or school, they often are tied to their
discipline and aren't comfortable interacting with those outside of the
discipline. In many ways, faculty members of various disciplines, such
as biology, physics, or those outside the sciences, speak different lan-
guages. At first glance this phenomenon may not seem like an issue,
but imagine being a student at a college or university where your professors rarely talk to each other about the classes you are taking. These
disciplinary divides can often trickle down to students, influencing
their perceptions of who may be available to support them. Our conversations with HBCU faculty members convinced us that talking
across the disciplines is essential to students' learning and ensures that

one aspect of the curriculum is not preventing students from being successful in another area of the curriculum.

Faculty members at Xavier University talk across disciplines. For example, because math is so integral to chemistry, it is essential that the chemistry faculty are in regular communication with the math faculty and that they are each fully aware of what is being taught to students and when. Faculty members understand that for students to be successful, their knowledge acquisition needs to be aligned and in sync. The kind of coordination at Xavier University requires the patience and time of faculty members. However, as Nydia, a faculty member, explains, "It's better for the students. They know they can go to anybody and I know exactly what they are covering in another professor's class. I know what they are required to know and what they don't need to know." Here we see one of the major differences between the ways that STEM majors are taught at these HBCUs as compared to many majority colleges and universities.[8] At the HBCUs, teachers are focused on what is best for students—what techniques, approaches, and strategies, and what will ensure that they learn. They place student needs over their own needs. At Xavier, which is a small, heavily research-based college, many faculty members are released from half of their teaching loads due to grant support, much like their counterparts at large research universities. However, unlike many of their research university peers, they see their role as half teaching and half research—and they see teaching as a complement to their research, not as a distraction from it.

Many of the faculty members with whom we talked at these HBCUs taught large classes without teaching assistants. At most research universities, classes with an enrollment above seventy-five students would have at least one teaching assistant. At the HBCUs, faculty members stay motivated by drawing upon their love of teaching and the excitement and motivation of the students in their classrooms. They spend considerable time ensuring that each of their students is successful, "holding their hands" along the way if necessary. Sally Ware, a chemistry professor at Xavier, shared with us: "I didn't coin this little phrase, but somebody did. It says, in general chemistry we hold both of their hands, and then whenever they get to organic, we only hold one of their hands. And . . . when they get to be Juniors, we drop their hands and let them do it on their own—that's a traditional course."

One of the things that we noticed at many of the HBCUs is a willingness to try new approaches when traditional ways of teaching were not working. At Morgan State University, for example, the engineering faculty members realized that their students perform better when they take math in the engineering department rather than in the math department. The difference between math courses in engineering departments and math in math departments is the difference between practice and theory. Engineering students inherently excel at solving problems of a practical nature, and the engineering math classes, crafted with this in mind, bolster the ability of students across all their classes. The theoretical nature of math taught in math departments can often work counter to the needs of engineering students. Unfortunately, most engineering programs in the United States require students to take their math classes in the math department, resulting in a mismatch in skills and a lack of communication between the departments around what students need for their major. The Morgan faculty members are not advocating that students do not take traditional math courses; however, they do not believe that using these courses as gatekeepers is advantageous to students.

The Morgan State University faculty members told us that things have changed in engineering, but in many schools the curriculum has not kept up to pace. In the past, engineers had to do the math required in the field by hand, but nowadays computers assist with most of the mathematical equations needed for engineering. Said one Morgan State professor, "We want our students to use math, but there's no need to memorize everything. We'd rather have them focus their efforts elsewhere." The Morgan State faculty members are open to changing the course of the curriculum to meet the needs of students entering the engineering workforce.

At Delaware State University, faculty members are working closely with the Center for Teaching and Learning and the School of Education on campus to "flip" their classrooms. Although it takes an enormous amount of time to make the classroom more interactive and to record videos of lectures for online learning, especially for those who are teaching four courses a semester, the Delaware State faculty members have witnessed the difference in student engagement when classes are interactive. Alice Wiley has recorded nearly 200 videos of herself teaching, so that students can learn hands-on from her *before* attending class. She then uses class time for students to apply that knowledge to exercises and projects. She also gives tests every week to ensure that students are well prepared for more significant exams. Given that most faculty members at these HBCUs do not have teaching assistants, they are putting in extra work to ensure that students learn and completely comprehend the course materials, with many grading on weekends to provide immediate feedback.

Lessons for Centering Students

For faculty members, prioritizing student needs over their own requires significant time, collaboration, openness to new and innovative teaching practices, and the patience to help students fulfill their potential to succeed. These are not generally characteristics of faculty at the colleges and universities our society lauds as "the best," but they are seen as fruitful attributes to a culture dedicated to mitigating disparities in racial achievement in STEM. These practices may seem radical because they can take time away from faculty research agendas. But if our colleges and universities work to create overall systemic change in STEM with a focus on students, these practices will become the norm.

First, imagine faculty who focus on teamwork over individuality and how that ethos might trickle down to the graduate students and undergraduates, changing the culture at an institution. What would happen in terms of student learning if faculty members chose to hire, not those who are focused on themselves, but instead the applicants who want to invest in students and would try any approach—retooling if needed, to ensure learning—as Xavier University's J. W. Carmichael did, year after year? What would happen in our colleges and universities if faculty members collaborate fully, working across disciplines and classes to ensure that we are doing the most to educate our students in STEM? It may seem daunting or even impossible for any institution to adopt these approaches. We recommend starting small with a subset of classes, particularly in the gateway courses, where students in STEM may require the most coordination and attention from faculty members.

Second, the faculty members at these HBCUs know that investment early on in students—such as literacy support, math boot camps, or remedial math classes—pays off in the end, because once students have the foundation on which to build their work, they will more likely prosper. Perhaps the most valuable lesson learned from these HBCUs is to look for the areas in which students fail or falter and, rather than blaming the students, come together as a faculty and change the environment that engenders failure. Faculty members who center students in their preparations for class, including innovative teaching approaches, are more likely to see students learn and thrive in STEM. We recommend revisiting areas where students have failed and reflecting on why they failed and what can be changed to ensure success—or, at the very least, put students on the pathway to success with additional support.

Prioritizing students' needs is at the core of increasing success for all students and is especially important with African American students, who are often marginalized in the STEM fields. To know inherently that their needs are central, and that their professors are willing to collaborate with them in taking responsibility for their learning process, is empowering and life-changing in creating the next generation of Black scientists.

6

Same-Gender, Same-Race Faculty
Role Models

ONE OF THE ADVANTAGES HBCUs have over their majority counterparts is the diversity of their STEM faculty members. In particular, there are higher numbers of African American professors. For instance, Black women make up 3 percent of the professoriate nationwide—18 percent of them are faculty members at HBCUs.[1] Most colleges and universities throughout the country have faculties that are predominantly White; nationally, 76 percent of the post-secondary teaching force is White. The lack of Black faculty and other faculty of color is particularly evident in the STEM fields. For example, in 2015, of all full-time faculty members at colleges and universities across the United States, including HBCUs and PWIs, Black men constituted only 2.5 percent in engineering, 1.4 percent in biological sciences, 1.8 percent in physical sciences, and 2.2 percent in mathematics.[2] Even more disappointing, Black women constituted only 1.4 percent of full-time STEM faculty members.[3] For instance, they constituted less than 1 percent in the field of biology, and 0.1 percent in mathematics. These are minuscule numbers and do not allow for Black students to be able to reliably find same-race, same-gender role models and mentors.

It is important to understand that the alignment of racial and gender backgrounds between students and faculty members matters in the learning and development of Black students in STEM. For instance, mentors with similar backgrounds and identities to their students can support them in myriad ways, including helping them to cope with racial and gender bias in the STEM pipeline, which can ultimately increase student confidence. Black students at HBCUs may also benefit from having role models who appreciate their perspectives and value their contributions to the STEM fields. Even if a faculty member is not African American, individuals who teach at HBCUs are more likely to be aware of and respectful toward the social circumstances that shape the intellectual and learning process of African Americans.[4]

As mentoring instills self-confidence, it can strengthen Black students' desire to pursue advanced degrees in the STEM fields. There is a serious need for the committed diversification of the STEM fields at majority institutions, a reevaluation and expansion of the definition of quality in faculty hiring processes, and the mentoring of more African Americans into the STEM faculty across the nation.

The Result of a Lack of Diversity

A lack of racial, ethnic, or gender diversity among faculty members is a barrier for African American students in STEM programs. This lack of diversity contributes to discrimination and stereotyping, as well as other attitudes that suggest that African American students do not belong in the STEM fields.[5] African American students at PWIs often experience racial microaggressions from students and faculty members.[6] These microaggressions, which are persistent racial slights, often manifest in the form of being viewed as angry and domineering rather than as learners and contributors to knowledge.[7] Although often dismissed, microaggressions can result in self-doubt, lower performance in the classroom, and mental health issues.

Within the context of the STEM fields, microaggressions around race and gender can occur among faculty members and students throughout the learning process. Often men will "huddle" together on research assignments and in labs and leave women out of the process.[8] Hardworking women, especially Black women, are often seen as bossy, whereas their male counterparts are seen as being in command.[9] In addition, both African American faculty members and students are subject to racial slurs and other hostile jokes, which create an unsupportive environment for learning.[10]

Research on HBCUs and the STEM fields suggests that having a same-race, and often same-gender, faculty mentor, combined with a culturally affirming environment, can serve as a counternarrative to Black students in STEM. Positive mentoring instills self-confidence and builds Black students' desire to pursue advanced degrees in the STEM fields.[11] Research also tells us that minority students who take multiple STEM courses with a professor of the same race are more likely to pursue a major in STEM.[12]

Because the STEM fields are not diverse in terms of student or faculty racial and gender makeup, classrooms can often be hostile environments for African Americans—recall Jesse's story in our Introduction to this book. Both research and anecdotes demonstrate that these students experience countless incidents of racism. African American students often feel dismissed by their professors, who seem to doubt their potential or that they belong in a STEM classroom. Often these students are not asked to contribute to classroom discussions and are left out of other class opportunities. For decades, research has demonstrated that African American students are often talked out of pursuing STEM degrees, are underestimated, and encounter STEM environments that send a strong message that they do not belong.

Benefits of Same-Race, Same-Gender Faculty Members

Not only is it inspiring for students to have faculty members that look like them and share the same cultural backgrounds and references, but it is important to have faculty members who understand their connections with students. Marge Hinton, a faculty member at North Carolina Central University, told us that she can relate to her students because she was one of them. "I came from the same background. I had the same developmental issues as many of them." Students note that having a Black woman in a position of leadership in the classroom makes a difference. According to Janet, a student at North Carolina Central:

> My teacher shared the statistics on Black women in science with me. One thing that she was telling me, when I was talking to her, was the decline in the amount of African American women that are involved in STEM. So that was something that really stood out to me, and I'm really big on statistics. A lot of people say I don't want to be a statistic in a negative way, but I do want to be a statistic in a positive

manner. So that's one thing that motivates me a lot, and just looking at my professor and seeing how well versed she is in everything. It's a good motivator and eye opener to have her. Seeing her motivates me. Seeing how well versed she is in the material and how much she knows is inspiring. And she looks like me. It's a good motivator and eye opener.

Similarly, Taylor, a senior studying biology at Xavier, said that her choice to pursue STEM was "really hard," but she also acknowledges that "it's going to be hard wherever you go." She identified a Black woman biology professor as playing a meaningful role in getting her to graduate. She also said that another Black woman biology professor who was her mentor was literally her best friend—"We are really close." Despite the fact that our nation has achieved gender parity at the baccalaureate level, serious efforts are needed to address the growing inequality and underrepresentation of Black women in STEM fields.

Faculty can have a meaningful presence in the lives of their students. Their motivation and commitment to students are shaped by their own personal life trajectories. For instance, a faculty member at Prairie View A&M University stated, "We're motivated to provide that face for them to let them know that they're needed in the field"—knowing that students thrive when those teaching them identify on measures of race or gender, and are sensitive to their own cultural backgrounds. Faculty members demonstrate awareness about how alignment of background can positively shape students' performances.

Several faculty members were also products of, and chose to begin their academic tenure at, an HBCU. Said one professor, "I selected this university and the biology department, one, because I was a product of it. And number two was that I could see I could do a lot. My contributions could probably be better here than at a majority university."

This faculty member understands the significance of his institution, as well as its needs, and it motivated him to return and give back. Another professor chose to teach at her current institution because she is a first-generation student and wanted to teach at an institution that was effective in serving students like her. "If I hadn't had that nurturing experience, I wouldn't have made it." The fact that these faculty members had themselves been educated at an HBCU offered the appropriate context in which to make sense of their actions for and interactions with students.

African American students are much more likely to do well in math and other STEM-related fields if they have exposure to role models and teachers of the same race.[13] Asha, an engineering student at Morgan State University, noted that coming to Morgan State was a shock in terms of what she saw in the classroom. She had attended a majority White high school and never had a science teacher, or any other teacher, who was not White. Morgan State gave her the experience of being taught by many African American professors with backgrounds similar to her own, and she found the experiences stimulating and inspiring. "I said to myself, there are actually Black professors out there that look like me." The same student found great satisfaction in having Black women as professors as well, telling us, "Diversity matters a lot in the classroom."

There are many differences in the ways African American teachers manage their classrooms and interactions with students.[14] And these differences play out in many HBCU environments as well. Whereas many White faculty members tend to focus on appropriate behavior in the classroom and following instructions, many African American professors are looking for ways students can co-construct learning and contributions to the classroom learning.[15]

Briana, a senior at North Carolina Central University, explained to us how important it was to have a Black woman teaching her math. "I can talk to her about anything. My personal issues, my class issues, and she understands me. I go to her office every day. I feel open with her. She knows me so well." Bernard chose to enroll at Prairie View A&M because he wanted to be surrounded by Black students and to be taught by Black faculty members. He shared that these factors were essential for his success and his development as a scholar: "When I came to do research, I saw so many people, and they were so educated and they were sophisticated, and I thought, 'I knew! I knew they were out there somewhere!' I wanted to go and surround myself with people who are kind of on the same mission as I was. That's what made me want to come here." Jackie, another student at Prairie View, said she felt that her professors understood what she was going through "because they have been through it before. They can relate."

Women tend to perform better in STEM courses when they are taught by women, even when they have been randomly assigned to these courses. Moreover, those women who come into college as high-achieving are much more likely to earn a STEM degree if they have a larger number of women teaching their STEM classes. At Xavier University, Black women students told us that seeing Black women teaching, as well as Black women alumni who are now doctors, was inspiring. Janelle mentioned, "It gets discouraging sometimes when I think about how long it takes to be a doctor, but when I see all these successful Black women, I feel motivated." Many students across the ten HBCUs that we visited told us that having same-race and same-gender role models was "inspiring" and "motivating," and helped to assure them that they "belonged on campus" and in a STEM degree program.

The Care of Non-Black Faculty Members

One of the major myths about HBCUs is that they do not have a diverse faculty. However, in reality, their faculties, are hugely diverse, with 43.7 percent of faculty members identifying as non-Black.[16] Significant numbers of faculty members at HBCUs are White (23.7 percent), Asian (9.5 percent), or Latino (2.4 percent), and many of these professors have chosen to teach at an HBCU because of the student focus and family environment.[17] During our interviews with students, they shared that although race-based role models are important, they also learn from, enjoy, and feel a great deal of care from non-Black faculty members. And those non-Black faculty members we talked with were equally as committed to students, cheering them on as they tackled challenges in STEM. They had a sense of empathy and understanding that, as faculty members, they have to engage the entire student and be open to all that they bring to the college experience. And many of the non-Black faculty members shared what they learned from their Black colleagues about engaging African American students in productive ways that enhance learning. They also understand where their limits are in terms of relating to students along racial lines.

One example of a non-Black faculty member making a considerable difference in the lives of HBCU students is Akil Toma, a professor of Middle-Eastern descent at Dillard University. As Dillard's lead faculty member in physics, Toma makes sure that the Black women professors and students in the physics department are surrounded by other Black women, asking Black female alumni to return to campus and discuss their pathways to the professoriate or other professions. He has also purposefully chosen to hire Black women faculty members in physics who earned their undergraduate degrees at Dillard to serve as role models for the students. He knows that he himself can bring the Black women at Dillard opportunities, but that they also need to have role models who look like them who can help them navigate the racism and sexism they will experience in college, graduate school, and the professoriate or other professions. Black women consistently face doubt about their place in STEM classrooms, both as students and faculty members.

At Huston-Tillotson University in Austin, Texas, students gravitate toward a White male professor who is dedicated to saving the environment. The professor, who is eccentric and full of energy, lived for a year in a converted dumpster on campus with minimal possessions and urges students to consume and use less in their daily lives. Students have a positive reaction to a student group he advises called "Green Is the New Black"—an effort to bridge the issues of race and sustainability. This widely known and liked professor is accepted by this mostly African American campus because of his willingness to be reflective and critical and to acknowledge his own privilege as a White man in the United States. Said the Huston-Tillotson professor,

> We have conversations about White privilege. I'm always having that conversation with myself and others because look at me. White male, first off, in the United States. Okay, most privileged person already on the planet. Then both my parents have a master's. I grew up in a middle-class, upper-middle-class neighborhood. Yeah, of course I have the opportunity to live on less in a dumpster. Not everybody, that is not an opportunity for everybody. It's kind of something that is not a necessity, to live in a dumpster, but some people don't have all those choices to have less.

The university president at the time of our study considered this faculty member popular among the students because he engaged them in innovative, hands-on approaches to environmental studies that cultivate lively discussion and sustained interest in STEM. But it is important to realize that this relationship he has with students would not exist if they had not first acknowledged and engaged in conversations about race and privilege. This built trust and rapport that made it easier for his students to learn from him.

At Morgan State University, engineering students told us that having Black professors was inspiring and helped them to see themselves as engineers in the future. However, they noted that they just want professors who care about them and help them learn. Students pointed to White professors who cared deeply and demonstrated that care in class and outside the classroom. Justin, one of the Morgan State students, when asked about his relationship with non-Black faculty members, shared that "all of the engineering faculty, even the White faculty, care about us, push us, and want us to succeed."

As we have noted, Xavier University is by far one of the most successful colleges in the nation at preparing future Black doctors. What's interesting about the institution is that the faculty are remarkably diverse. In fact, many of the faculty members in the biochemistry department, which prepares the future doctors, are non-Black. Although students value their relationships with the Black faculty members and understand the motivational factors in those relationships, they were clear that non-Black faculty members can provide just as much support and that the students do not feel that their relationships are less than those with Black faculty members or that the non-Black faculty members see them differently. A few small studies of non-Black faculty members at HBCUs show the majority of them are inclined toward justice and believe that African American students have enormous potential.[18]

Those non-Black faculty members with whom we interacted spoke positively about their experiences, cherished the HBCU environment, and thoroughly enjoyed their relationships with students. They demonstrated a large amount of pride in their students and had a sense of what the students had overcome to be at the institution. In other words, non-Black faculty members are shaped by an HBCU culture that centers the Black student experience, which comes from cultivating a stronger sense of empathy for their students that is tangible and can be felt in the interactions with them. They work to relate to their students, to get to know them, to understand the extent and influence of their backgrounds and experiences, and to discover what motivates them to succeed.

Lessons for Colleges and Universities

African American students are more likely to be engaged and learn when they have African American faculty members who reflect their experiences, passions, and cultural backgrounds. Even those faculty members who are not African American, but have a commitment to the success of African Americans, can make a fundamental difference in the lives and futures of these students. Of note, all students would benefit from having access to faculty who share common experiences and cultural reference points as well as access to those who do not. The beauty of a rich learning environment is to feel nurtured and safe while also being challenged to learn new things and work to your best ability. Having a diverse faculty is the only way to ensure this kind environment for all students to succeed.

HBCUs can teach us a considerable amount about hiring a diverse faculty across myriad types of colleges and universities. These institutions are open to hiring faculty members from a variety of institutions and realize that teaching and research talent as well as care for students can be found in graduates from many different types of research universities. All too often, PWIs fetishize only a few research institutions, and due to explicit or implicit bias, when they are hiring new faculty, they dismiss applicants with degrees from other research institutions as not being rigorous or academically respectable. The HBCUs in this study looked beyond just formal credentials and more closely at an individual applicant's potential to contribute to the school's historic mission and culture of centering Black student success.[19]

First, colleges and universities must consider creating a broader definition of quality in hiring new faculty members. Because African Americans and HBCUs have been the victims of discrimination, they are more open to wider definitions of quality in hiring processes—quality beyond who someone's mentor is, their publication record, and the ranking of the institution from which they hail. The HBCUs in our study are interested in what faculty members can bring to the faculty in addition to their research skills—attributes including creativity, generosity, and care, as demonstrated through commitment to advising and teaching, that can make a profound difference in students' lives. The nation's other colleges and universities would benefit from modeling their hiring practices on the more open practices of HBCUs and other Minority Serving Institutions, which look for a multitude of talents rather than focusing only on prestige.[20] What would happen if colleges and universities more generally were open to a variety of definitions of quality and emphasized hiring faculty who bring the greatest benefit to students? What if a demonstrated respect for diversity were a fundamental component in faculty hiring? When faculties are more diverse, as they are at HBCUs, there are fewer of the microaggressions that lead faculty members and students to leave STEM fields.[21]

Second, these HBCUs are more likely to hire faculty members that are community-oriented, committed to the greater institution over their own individualistic needs, and focused on student achievement and success. These factors make a considerable difference in STEM achievement and were evident during our interviews with HBCU faculty members. The faculty members who have control over the tenure system should consider tweaking the faculty reward structure to encourage faculty members to include research and teaching opportunities that engage or promote new practices or programs for student learning. So often these responsibilities are given to staff, and although they are dedicated to student achievement, faculty members are in the best position to identify and understand the challenges and needs of their students. Faculty members hold immense authority and influence in the academy. They should bridge this divide with staff and work closely with them across student and academic affairs. Student experiences and outcomes are a result of a multitude of overlapping factors inside and outside the classroom. Faculty members with a community orientation toward student achievement in STEM will find greater support in addressing the challenges that hinder their students.

Third, colleges and universities should consider providing all faculty members, especially those who identify as non-Black, the opportunity to learn about the history and contemporary issues of Black education in America. Efforts to improve the racial and gender representation in STEM faculties are slowly becoming more common across our nation, but it will be sometime before the composition of the academy drastically changes. Until it does, institutions should make every effort to help current faculty members acknowledge their biases in teaching and mentorship so that they can begin addressing any behavior that may discourage the learning of Black and other minority students.

Fourth, although the percentage of faculty members who are African American is far higher at these HBCUs than at majority colleges and universities, it is possible for majority institutions to capitalize on the strength of a diverse faculty and for faculty members to have a belief in the potential of all students. The first step is recruiting diverse faculty who are committed to the success of all students, including African American students. If faculty members do not have this commitment in their teaching and mentorship, why are they hired? How can they fit into an institution that claims to be focused on and committed to student success for African Americans in STEM? These are the types of questions we need to ask ourselves if we say we care about the success of African American students in STEM fields.

These HBCU environments cannot be duplicated on majority campuses, but these other colleges and universities can draw from HBCU successes. Although the kind of faculty diversity present at these HBCUs is not likely to happen at majority institutions at a rapid pace, faculty members in STEM throughout the nation can believe in the success of their African American students and see them as future scientists like the professors at these HBCUs do. The HBCUs in our study dispel the myth that success in STEM fields is only for those who are naturally gifted and is not a product of hard work. African American students who have the curiosity and drive to succeed are too often steered away from careers in science due to these persistent and pernicious myths.[22]

7

A Culture of Family

I actually fell in love with Lincoln because of the family-oriented environment . . . you have people out here having the same goal as you, and they want to see you do better.

—Janet, biology student, Lincoln University

When I came here, everyone accepted me, made me feel like part of the family, they didn't make me feel like an outsider.

—Eddie, physics student, Dillard University

JANET AND EDDIE ARE DESCRIBING what we consider a culture of family. Despite the many differences in the institutions—Lincoln is medium-size public university located right outside Philadelphia, and Dillard is a small private, university in New Orleans—the cultures in their STEM programs are similar. At HBCUs, students' relationships with their faculty and fellow students are imbued with a powerful feeling of kinship, which can help explain why HBCUs are so effective at graduating students in the sciences.

Many Black communities consider HBCUs to be safe havens where Black students can learn, grow, and be empowered by their own communities. These schools have deep historical roots in elevating and building up Black communities by helping them pave their own path toward self-determination and by actively caring for one another and for each other's children; the achievement of a single child is considered an achievement for the whole community.[1] This ideology has been carried forward since the inception of HBCUs in the early nineteenth century, and it remains evident in how students and faculty members characterize the learning environment in STEM. As has been the case down through the years at HBCUs, perceiving their community as a family nucleus strengthens faculty members' sense of obligation to student learning, and fashions students' perceptions of achievement as a collective endeavor. For Jazmyne, a physics junior at Dillard, "The fact that it's built on family, family-like traditions, and the fact that everybody is supposed to be together, or work together, it helps out, because if you're by yourself, you're not able to [learn]."

A culture of family counters the dominant view of the role of higher education and expectations for students.[2] The dominant view is that college is a journey of self-discovery, where students, on their own, identify their passions and secure the resources and experiences to cultivate them, in order to find their purpose in life. This popular narrative presupposes that students themselves possess and employ these values. Faculty members create the academic standards for achievement, give weekly lectures, provide research opportunities, and hold office hours. Students, on their own, must decide the best course of action to meet those standards, to secure those opportunities, to take advantage of those office hours, and, ultimately, to succeed. This certainly holds true for learning in the sciences at those colleges.[3] HBCUs provide a different learning environment, where, in the spirit of a familial bond—an orientation toward community well-being[4]—shared by students and faculty members, students can more successfully meet those same standards. At the HBCUs we visited, we found that the shape of the journey to earning a STEM degree is no different from other institutions, but how students walk their path, with their family of faculty and peers, ultimately makes a difference in their sense of belonging on campus and in their performance in the classroom.

Faculty Members as Family

"Fictive kinship"—the idea that you can be kin to people who are not your blood relations—structures how the HBCU faculty members in our study understood their roles and responsibilities as educators.[5] They often saw students as their own "children" and felt compelled to actively ensure their success in the sciences. The perception of students as children was not about immaturity, but about the amount of energy and resources faculty members were willing to deploy for their students. For instance, faculty members made the effort to get to know their students—not just their names but their backgrounds and day-to-day challenges. This allowed them to build trust and rapport and closely monitor student progress. For students with difficulty making the transition to college, this level of acknowledgment and effort from faculty members made them feel that they belonged, that achievement in college and in science was an attainable goal. Oftentimes, challenges to student success were met with fierce intervention by faculty members, who expanded their roles and responsibilities to students beyond the classroom. Here, we share with you the stories of five faculty members—Lynette Shaw, Thomas Owens, Rachel Waters, Akil Toma, and Samantha Bass—that best illustrate how the culture of family shapes their approaches to support students.

Lynette Shaw is a professor and the chair of the biology department at Prairie View A&M University. For Shaw, seeing her department, both students and faculty members, as a family unit requires a foundation of acknowledgment and trust. As the lead faculty member in her department, making the effort to meet and learn about her students is the initial step in cultivating a culture of family:

> We have over 500 [students in the biology department]. I know 90 percent of them by their first names. And that makes a difference when you start, when you can see a student and you call them by their first name. I tell mine right off . . . "Tell me your name, give me an opportunity to learn your name so that when I see you I can speak to you. If I don't know your name, if you see me, walk up to me, introduce yourself to me." It means something when you let a student know that you are trying to learn their name. And if [I] forget it, I say to them, "Would you please tell me your name again. Not only do I want you to know who I am, but I want to know who you are too, because you're very important to me. Your success is my success."

Making the effort to learn each student's name is a critical form of acknowledgment that can help students feel valued. Black students in STEM at other colleges often report that their science classes do not affirm their presence.[6] Across the country, students of color often find themselves in situations where racial biases fashion how faculty members acknowledge and treat them. When a professor, such as Shaw, wishes to learn a student's name, it can change how they feel about their class or their major. They are no longer "a number." Learning a student's name, and acknowledging students by name when they are present, humanizes the learning experience and offers the opportunity that faculty members need to build the kind of relationship that allows them to effectively support their students. Said Shaw:

> I take every effort I can to learn the names of my students so when I see them. . . . If they haven't done something, I will call their hand on it and say, "It was reported to me that you didn't do this. You need to come to my office so I can talk with you so we can see what happened." That is showing them early on that you care for them. [With] my upper-classmen, I stay on them too.

The value of learning a student's name includes more than the benefit of acknowledgment; it includes acting on this acknowledgment. Learning their names and remembering them, taking "every effort," allows Shaw to identify her students should she receive unfavorable information about them. Her reach is amplified by the more senior students, who most likely have benefited from Shaw's approach early on in their tenure at Prairie View A&M. In this way, she can immediately address student challenges, demonstrating to students that she cares about their progress and that her decisions most likely are made with their best interests in mind.

Once ties and trust are established between faculty members and students, a culture of family provides the means to motivate and guide them. Shaw arrived at Prairie View in 1991 and took on the role of chair in 2006. Regarding the departmental culture she helped build over those years, she hopes her students will say about the department: "This is like my home. This is my family. I've got to make sure that I'm on point with them. I don't want to do anything to embarrass them because they know at the end of the day everything they're doing is for my good." Helping students understand their community in the biology department as a "family" motivates them to be "on point," or to be at their very best. In fact, the notion of family pushes students to draw parallels between their faculty members and their parents or guardians—people in their lives whom students tend to want to make proud when those individuals exert energy and resources to help them succeed. But more importantly for Shaw, cultivating this culture can be a continuation of what her students understand and value in their home life:

> They really buy into it, and they realize that's not only showing them compassion and that you care for them . . . that's showing them a family kind of love that when they leave home they realize, "I may not be at home, but this is just like someone in my family staying on me, saying, 'Okay, you can do this.'"

For Black students the adjustment to college can be especially challenging when what they value is not mirrored in their classes, department, or university. Finding themselves in a "family" culture from the first moment they arrive at Prairie View A&M, where faculty and other students care about them and want them to succeed, can turn that adjustment into an immediately affirming experience: "We want [them] to be successful. At the end of the day the students realize how much we care, and it makes them want to propel to the highest level that they can, to go even beyond the limits of the sky." Conceiving of the biology department as a family allows students to more easily develop connections that help forge trust in their faculty. This trust is met and maintained by action, where faculty actively shape the conditions of their students' success.

Students often know where they want to be, but have little idea on how to get there. This challenge was the case for many of the students we met with. They were intelligent, hardworking, and persevering, but aside from knowing that they had to study and do well in their courses, they were not sure how to manage other aspects that would be significant in their learning and progression. Considering the students in the biology department as her family, Shaw, like any parent who wishes her children to reach their goals, is actively shaping her students' paths. Take Rebecca, a sophomore who was having difficulty figuring out which courses she had to take to satisfy both her degree requirements and the prerequisites for medical school:

> Professor Shaw checks in on us. She makes sure we have everything. I actually have a meeting with her at 3:00 today to go over my degree plan. . . . When I was setting up the meeting, I was like, "I know you're probably busy. We can do it whenever you're available." She was like, "Okay, when are you available?" I set up the meeting on Friday and she told me she could get me in on Monday. I was willing to wait a couple of weeks or whenever she was available. She just fit me into her schedule.

There was no waiting with Shaw. Despite Rebecca's willingness to "wait a couple of weeks," Shaw wants her students to be successful. Degree planning is stressful when the courses in one's major that are needed in order to pursue one's intended profession don't clearly line up with general university course requirements. Mapping out curriculum for the remainder of a student's time in the program can require counseling by a faculty member. This usually has to be done early on so that the student is on track to reach her goals, because decisions related to coursework can have implications for future opportunities (such as internships and research). Knowing the urgency and implication of mapping out one's courses, Shaw wanted to meet with Rebecca on the next available workday.

Sam, a senior, is getting ready to apply to medical school. He recalls that early in his freshmen year, Shaw, aware of his desire to pursue the medical profession, sought him out to inform him of a summer opportunity that provides "academic enrichment" for students interested in careers in medicine or dentistry. This opportunity allowed him to learn early on about effective strategies for medical school admissions and to build important ties with faculty members and staff at some of the nation's prestigious universities. In describing Shaw's role, Sam explained how attending Prairie View A&M University prepared him for the future:

> Just through the connection with Dr. Shaw . . . telling me about the program and getting into the program . . . being so close-knit and family oriented here in the biology department . . . the faculty helps you get your foot in the door of a whole lot of places that I feel like I probably wouldn't have gotten at another university.

Applying to medical school takes much more than submitting an application. It requires building a competitive application—including excellent performance in the prerequisite courses, preparing for and taking the MCAT exam, and securing experiences and opportunities to demonstrate interest in and commitment to the practice of medicine. This process usually begins early on in a student's college career. Students who start focusing on this later in college might not have sufficient time to prepare, making it much less likely that they will be admitted to a medical school. Because of Shaw's watchful eye and penchant for knowing and tracking her students' progress, Sam was introduced to this summer opportunity. He attributes his success to the "close-knit" relationship with Shaw and the faculty members, which led him to receive benefits that he believes he would not have received at another university.

Thomas Owens, also a professor at Prairie View A&M, is known as the "biology patriarch," a "father figure" in the department. Like Shaw, he has an approach to helping students learn and succeed that is driven by the sort of closeness that exists in a strong family unit. Since his arrival on campus nearly four decades ago, Owens has dedicated his life to increasing the representation of Black students in the sciences and health professions. In fact, he keeps a list of the students he has taught who are now successful doctors—they now number over 500. He has succeeded in achieving this goal in part because of the quality of his engagement with students and how he marries the learning of content with life skills. Student recollection of his approach to teaching illustrates the family mentality that shapes the culture in their department.

Even at 75 years of age, Owens's dedication to his students has not diminished. Students we talked with mentioned his tireless efforts to be available and to make sure they had what they needed to succeed.[7] For Rebecca, after a series of classes, her typical day might end with an evening study session with her classmates. Midterms and final exams determine a large part of final course grades, and study sessions offer students a last-minute opportunity to review and problem-solve together. Although faculty members are not responsible for teaching beyond their formal classroom lectures, Owens does what he believes is the best for his students, including being present to help out at their late-night study sessions. Rebecca noted, "I think just being able to talk to your professors is so big, and having professors that come in for study sessions, like Professor Owens being there from 6:00 to 9:00. I thought for sure one of these days his wife was going to walk in and yell at us for keeping him away. He's always there for us." Attending a semester of three-hour study sessions is like adding an additional course to one's teaching load. Andy, a student in these study sessions, said Owens does this because a student's success in one single course has consequences for subsequent ones:

> He would come after hours, it would 7:00 P.M. or 8:00 P.M. He would be here with us until like 9:00 P.M. He would come back and have the study group with us and just answer any questions we had about the material. He wanted to make sure that we learned everything possible about general biology. That's the backbone of all of the courses that we're taking. We're in genetics now.

By increasing his availability to students, Owens offers them the chance to improve their scores on their exams and to solidify their knowledge of the concepts needed to master more complex topics. Given his many other university responsibilities, it shows real care and commitment to spend additional time in the evenings to see his students through their science courses. He is not always available for the study sessions, but he teaches his students early on the benefits of studying together.

Jake, a sophomore in the department, described how nervous he was in his first year at Prairie View A&M University. He was nervous about the transition to college and how he would hold up in his science classes, since the sciences had a reputation for difficulty and competitiveness. But his fears calmed down when he met Owens:

I came here, and Professor Owens made everything a little more comfortable for me. Professor Owens started pointing out different people and [he'd] tell us . . . "These are your classmates" . . . "You guys are going to be a family. When you guys have study groups, make sure you have three people together, and you guys focus on the material that I'm teaching you guys, but also make sure that you guys go out sometimes together and have fun together and do everything together." This gave me a better environment and family bond with everybody.

Owens pushed back against Jake's fears about learning in the sciences by encouraging him to study together with other students, which would give Jake "a better environment." By grouping his students together and calling them a family, Owens created a group dynamic that addressed the challenges to learning and succeeding in the sciences. These dynamics were to be maintained both inside and outside the classroom. Chiming into the conversation, Joel, a sophomore, shared:

The biology, well, we have kind of the same hashtag. It's called #TeamBio . . . the biology department is kind of like a family. We'll study together; we mostly eat together in the commons. We go out together. Even when we party—and Professor Owens will vouch for this. He'll say, "Don't go to all those frat parties and this and that. If you party, you party with Team Bio and that's it." We have our own Team Bio parties with only biology majors . . . to stay structured. We all have common goals. We're like-minded. We're not going to be out all hours of the night, 3:00 or 4:00 in the morning, coming back intoxicated. No, we're going to come back and study after the party. . . . You're going to see most of your study buddies at the party anyway so you're going to have fun, you're going to get your work done. It's all solid.

The notion of family guides how students interact and relate to each other. It provides community during challenges related to coursework and to campus life overall. By promoting community among his students—#TeamBio—especially those with similar educational and professional goals, Owens created a system in which students care for each other and hold each other accountable, a structure in which their social choices are first and foremost aligned with their academic priorities. When manifested in group dynamics, it can be a powerful tool to ensure that learning conditions maximize student achievement in the sciences and discourage the attrition of students. Sarah's thoughts demonstrate how a family unit can help save students from leaving the sciences:

You know when freshmen first come into college . . . [they] are just trying to party. They're like, "I'm finally in college and it's time to turn up." They're not realizing that if you party every day, all day, day in and day out, that you're not going to get to your books. You're going to be missing class because you're maybe like hung over from the day before. I feel like that's how the freshmen get weeded out. When you come to college, the upperclassmen for biology are looking at you like, "Hey, you can't do all that partying. You have to be with us." They kind of like take you under their wing, and they're like, "You need to come to New Science tonight and study." Then after like the hard tests are over . . . then they party as a family.

Learning and working together offers numerous benefits to address challenges related to the transition to college and the adjustment to higher academic standards, especially in the sciences. Student achievement in the department of biology is driven by the interdependent values of community or being attentive to the needs of others. This phenomenon is captured by the notion of family, an ideal that Owens actualizes daily in his work.

Performing well in the sciences takes a great deal more effort than cracking a book and burning the midnight oil. When Owens envisions his students' success, his scope of vision moves beyond the confines of the school and into the realm of the workforce. A high sense of professionalism is just as important to Owens as learning the concepts in the biology text. When we asked Andy, a sophomore in the biology department and an aspiring physician, how he would describe Owens's method for preparing students for medical school, he shared:

> He just doesn't allow us to be unprofessional in his classes. He would call you out in a minute. Even just the way you present yourself in class and dress. I wouldn't dare go to his class sagging my pants because I know him, and I know what he would tell me. He might not tell me during class, but he might bring me aside after class and say, "Look man, you need to dress more appropriately." . . . His whole goal, his whole mindset, is getting us in the professional school, in the professional world. He tries to get us acclimated to that—speaking correctly and dressing correctly. He does put in the time and the effort to try to groom us like professionals. I'm thankful for him because I've learned so much from him.

Owens knows that "sagging pants" would be inappropriate dress for the research labs and hospitals where his students want to find future employment. Using class time to address these issues is not frivolous, for students need to build their sense of professionalism. In fact, it can be as fundamental as being on time, explained Andy:

> The first time I was late to his class, I had put my phone on silent that night. I went to sleep, and I wake up and look at my phone and it's 10:00. I was like, "Oh my gosh." When I walked into the class, he says, "Andy, where have you been?" I just said, "Oh, Professor Owens, I overslept." He was like, "Well, set your alarm." I said, "I don't have one." He said, "What?! You don't have an alarm?" He was literally about to drive me to Walmart during his lunch break to get an alarm clock. But I talked to him afterward and I was like, "I'll go get one. I promise I'll go get one tonight." I've learned now. I've learned now. I'm fine.

In the "professional world" that awaits his students, success can depend on how one presents oneself. Being on time, learning to manage one's time, is such an important lesson to learn that, as Andy put it, Owens was ready to drive Andy to the store to buy an alarm clock. Strong grades can help students access future educational opportunities, but how long they can walk that path is often determined by how well students understand the values and norms that are privileged in professional occupations and spaces. Owens's actions in the classroom are a testament to that reality and an example of how faculty members will do for their students what they will do for their own children.

Rachel Water is on the staff in the academic advising services, and a lecturer, at Huston-Tillotson University in Austin, Texas. In her role, she works closely with students in the sciences—monitoring their academic progress and helping them balance their obligations—with the hopes that they "leave HT with a stronger sense of who they are, the world they live in, and more grounded in how they go about living their life." When it comes to being an effective support for them in their science courses, she believes, as Shaw does, that knowing the students and spending time with them is often the best means to address their challenges. "I know every single thing about my students. Sometimes it's TMI." "TMI"—too much information—is information of a personal nature that is usually shared only with a person one is close to. That is how well Water knows her students—to the level of TMI. This allows her to "care like a mother." We asked her to expand on what that means for students in STEM:

> You show real concern. It's not just pass-my-class concern. It's a genuine I-want-to-see-you-be-successful concern about all the things they do. With my students that are athletes, I always make a game. I don't care what I have to do. If it's a Saturday or Sunday—and sometimes it's hard because I have children of my own—but I make a game. . . . Whatever sports my students play, I'm going to be there to support, to show them that I support more than just their academic accomplishments but their athletic and their outside-of-class [accomplishments.] I want them to know that even if no one else cares about what they're doing, I do. Some of their parents are so far away, they just can't be there, or their parents work all the time. I just feel that it's very important to foster that family environment, that family feel, so when they're away from home they still have a home.

Being a "mother" to her students is more than just expressing a sense of care for their well-being, but an actual, consistent demonstration of care. For her student athletes, a few of whom struggle with balancing their academic and athletic obligations, attending their games is an opportunity to showcase her support, especially when those they are close with, such as parents or guardians, are unable to attend. Water wants her students to feel that when they are at Huston-Tillotson, they are in fact "home." Creating that home, or "family environment," also helps Water monitor and facilitate a student's progress. Water recalled a case where developing an understanding of a student's activities gave her an opportunity to intervene when a student did not make his tutoring session:

> If Christopher doesn't show up for his tutoring—call me! When you call me, I'm going to call his coach, and between me and his coach, this is something he does to not want to deal with. He doesn't want to have to deal with me. . . . If I call his coach, practice is going to be a nightmare. So, in turn we put them to the fire. "This is what you want? Okay. I'm going to put you in place. I'm going to bring you to the water. And now drink it, and we won't have any problems. Don't drink it and then we'll see what happens from there." . . . These students care about what they see you do, which is why, again, going to the basketball games. He's a basketball player. He knows that if he doesn't do what he's supposed to do, he can't play. If I come to the game, and you're not playing, we have a problem—because that means you didn't do something, so now you have to tell me what's going on. I have access to your grades, so if you're not doing well, you can't lie.

That level of intervention is based on the quality of care Water provides to her students. By demonstrating her support for Christopher's athletic career, she can build social ties with his coach, which gives her credence to work in tandem with the coach to keep Christopher on his academic path. When a family environment is promoted, challenging students can be met with less resistance because the intention comes from a place of love and commitment rather than solely of professional obligation.

The approaches of Lynette Shaw, Thomas Owens, and Rachel Water best illustrate how faculty members across our ten HBCUs teach, mentor, and support their students in the sciences. Coming from a place of family, in which they see their students as being like their own children, they are able to actively engage and shape their students' pathways. But more importantly, this approach demonstrates how the challenge to student achievement in the sciences is less concerned with mastering the content and more with the conditions in which students thrive. Take, for instance, Samantha Bass, a faculty member in the physics department at Dillard University, where she had earned her bachelor's degree. Her story demonstrates what happens when faculty express family-like obligation and care for their students.

When we met with Bass, she was just completing her first year as a tenure-track assistant professor in the physics department. We asked her how she had arrived at her current post. Bass grew up in New Orleans, where she attended a Catholic high school that cultivated her interest in STEM. Choosing Dillard to continue her education, Bass had little idea back then how that decision would pave a way toward opportunities that few women, let alone Black women, find themselves in front of. "I entered Dillard and went straight into the Louis Stokes Alliances for Minority Participation Program (LSAMP). And I was under the supervision of Doctor Akil Toma." LSAMP is a program funded by the National Science Foundation that supports the achievement of racial minorities in STEM.[8] This program gave Bass space and time outside of class to explore her burgeoning interest in physics. In her first year, when students are heavily influenced by their peers and the popular beliefs and opinions they hold, Bass felt a tension between her attraction to the sciences and the stereotype that it was impossible for a Black woman to get a physics degree. She lauded the program for cementing her academic trajectory in physics: "The LSAMP program actually set a great foundation . . . it was a great introduction. That experience, I could say, kind of propelled me into research." Participation also laid the foundation for a meaningful relationship with Professor Toma, whose approach to teaching and mentorship Bass greatly benefited from.

Toma, whom we introduced earlier in this book, recognizes that solutions to the enduring inequality of opportunity for Black women in STEM. Achievement takes a great deal more than mastering its content. Students need to be recognized and affirmed, by faculty members and professional researchers, as members of the STEM community.[9] Like any community, STEM has a set of cultural norms, practices, and traditions that so often define as successful those who recognize and abide by them. For Toma, his primary work was to offer that insight to students like Bass—to teach them how to successfully navigate, and to establish their belongingness in, the STEM community. Bass noted:

> Professor Toma made sure we had experience, and when I say "we," all of us who were interested in doing projects, all of the physics majors here, he encouraged us to participate in mentoring, participate in tutoring; provided exposure with other people, other researchers, and what the rest of the

world is doing. So, I got to travel to different conferences and present my work, and getting that taste of it, exposure to what the rest of the country was doing. . . . So, I would say that my experience here at Dillard was unlike any other.

Toma's mentorship did not end there. He continued to teach Bass the value of these activities, how these experiences are connected to her achievement in physics, and how to capitalize and build on each opportunity to further her trajectory. Toma brought to light the "rules of the game," the unspoken norms and practices that are so often expected of students despite any limitations of their background and home life. He kept in touch with her throughout her time at Dillard and beyond, extending that light even in the midst of one of our country's worst natural disasters: Hurricane Katrina.

In 2005, Bass's final year at Dillard, Hurricane Katrina ripped through the states of Louisiana, Alabama, and Mississippi, killing nearly 2,000 people and displacing thousands of individuals and families. New Orleans bore the brunt of this disaster. A majority of its residents were Black and low-income. Many were unable to escape the wrath of the hurricane, and many did not have the means to rebuild after it abated. For the communities of New Orleans, Hurricane Katrina was more than a natural disaster. It was an event that revealed decades of the city's having ignored the dilapidated conditions of these residential areas, and having failed to make renovations and improvements to infrastructure that could have prevented the mass destruction of these communities. The Black communities and institutions of New Orleans are primarily located below sea level, so they were hit the hardest by the flooding that overcame the city, leaving them in worse condition than before. Dillard University was flooded, and its students had to be transferred to other schools for the semester. Bass was sent to the University of

Arkansas in Pine Bluff. "I tried to attend UAPB during that semester. It didn't work out. I actually stayed out a semester."

The aftermath of Hurricane Katrina presented significant personal challenges to her academic progress. Even after she returned to New Orleans and re-enrolled at Dillard, "It was a balancing act." While she and her family lived in a trailer as they were rebuilding their home, Bass registered for triple the normal credit hours so that she could graduate on time. She also took on two demanding research internships at a stem-cell lab and a gene therapy lab, and tried to discern her next steps for advanced education. Along this pathway, Toma was always in sight, offering Bass the guidance she needed to complete her degree:

> Toma was still mentoring me throughout the entire time. I would go to him because there were times when I was pre-empting going into medical school, or applying for an MD-PHD Program, or just PHD. I just . . . couldn't make up my mind what I wanted to do. And he put me in connection with people who could help along the way.

Five years later, Bass went on to earn her PhD in biomedical science from Tulane University. "He is an awesome mentor . . . it's rare that you find people that you want to just keep that connection for years throughout your career," she shared. Quoted in an article by the Associated Press, Toma stated, "I believe in women, especially minority women. . . . They are not less than anybody else. Just give them the chance and they will be the best. Give them what they need, and they will do." He does not buy into the stereotype that women are inherently unfit for the sciences, but in fact argues the reverse—that the problem lies in the extent to which the culture of science, its members, and everyday practices acknowledge and offer the tools and proper conditions to women of color to fully realize their potential and talents. Similar to his counterparts at Prairie View A&M and Huston-Tillotson, Toma's commitment to Bass, to his students, extends far beyond what is commonly expected of faculty members. It is a commitment not only to his students' well-being in the class, but to their well-being in life. When Bass returned to Dillard as a faculty member, she sought to replicate this very ideal, hoping to influence students in the same way.

Students enter college with perceptions of their abilities and potential. They often, however, allow negative rumors about challenging or difficult coursework or degree pathways to deter them from pursuing fruitful opportunities. In teaching and working with students, Bass aims to dispel such rumors and discourage that thinking to continue among them:

> I give them my background and they're like, "Wow, geez. I could never." And the first thing I say is, "Don't . . . never say never. Nothing is too difficult for you, it's just the way you perceive it." That makes the difference. Students enter in with that fear, or they have a bad introduction to something, and it sets the tone for the way that they perceive it for a long time. And so, my job is to break those boundaries, to break that wall down, at least work at it as much as I can, just by starting off with examples, using myself as an object, using small things—using a can of soda, for an example—looking at things in a different light, and understanding that physics describes everything around you. So being able to describe that gives you power. It's not something for you to fear. It just gives you power.

Changing students' perceptions takes more than merely telling them the opposite of what they believe. It also requires demonstrating the fallacy of those fears. As someone who had recently and successfully walked the pathway to earn a PhD, Bass understands firsthand what it might take to convince students of their talents and capacity to succeed. In her approach to teaching, it means helping her students perceive the content differently or informing them of the ubiquity of "physics"—that everyday life is shaped by its principles. By reframing how students conceive of learning in STEM, Bass aims to disempower whatever underlies students' fears. "[Toma] told me, 'It's time for you to learn about the significance of where you are and who you can be.' . . . That conversation helped me to stay on track. It opened up my eyes in terms of understanding what was out there."[10] In turn, Toma embodies the institutional values of family that drive the many ways students are acknowledged, embraced, and supported at these HBCUs. His work with Bass aimed to change her perceptions of who she is allowed to be in society, to reveal her capacity to actualize her passion for STEM. Although the time and effort that faculty members commit to their students seem extraordinary—some would even say unnecessary—it is important to note that these faculty members have only a few years to push back against and undo years of students internalizing a belief that they themselves are the barrier to success.

Lessons Learned from the Family

As we have seen, notion of family helps explain the achievements of Black students at HBCUs. It is also a powerful reminder to those outside that learning and achieving in STEM are not solely defined by a culture of personal gain. In fact, a culture of family helps battle the challenges that infect the communities and minds of our Black students—the belief in their inferiority in society, the devaluation of their histories and backgrounds, and the poor quality of the K–12 systems that underprepare them for higher education. We believe that institutions and programs in STEM can draw inspiration from how these HBCUs succeed in producing the next generation of scientists and health professionals.

First, faculty members should spend time getting to know their students. We understand that faculty members at larger institutions, where lectures can hold hundreds of students, may have a more difficult time learning and engaging with their students. One of the most effective ways to minimize this distance is to work closely with staff who are committed to help students succeed both inside and outside the classroom. It is important to remember that student learning does not happen in a vacuum. Students are very much affected by their own circumstances, which can either encourage or constrain the quality of their effort for a given class. Also, consider recruiting more senior students to work with newer students, in order to create a wide web that gives you some sense of how your students are doing.

Second, students benefit when faculty members structure assignments and exams to be more group-oriented and collaborative. Recent research by social psychologists and physicists suggests that reframing assessments from an individual to a collective endeavor can improve an individual's learning.[11] Increasing opportunities for collaboration, such as peer instruction and cooperative problem solving, have been known to reduce achievement disparities for underrepresented groups in STEM. Doing so also encourages students to develop working relationships and the penchant to learn from others as opposed to struggling on their own. Faculty should refrain from creating and reinforcing environments that pit students against each other, as this helps no one.

Third, faculty members should group together students with similar goals and cultivate a family-oriented environment, where their social choices align with their academic priorities. So often institutions continue to arrange themselves in ways that separate the academic from the social. What if students no longer had to choose? For students at Prairie View A&M University, working in groups helped them find a balance, to work hard without the cost of losing opportunities to have fun.

A culture of family can be viewed as weak or unfitting for disciplines considered economically fruitful and prestigious, like those in STEM. Somehow a narrative of personal effort and competitiveness—followed by practices that reinforce these values—is more acceptable in our society in allocating opportunities among students. And yet this narrative reveals the irony of our society's logic: We wish for more racial diversity—among students and faculty—in the STEM disciplines and workforce, but we do not want to alter or change the rules of the game. In Chapter 8 we offer an agenda to begin solving this conflict.

8

An Agenda for the Future of STEM

AS WE WRITE THIS BOOK, the United States is in racial unrest, with more overt racial slights and aggressions becoming more frequent and a federal effort to weaken the enforcement of civil rights in full swing.[1] In the midst of this environment, African American students are set to attend college or return to college, many pursuing degrees in the STEM fields. We have a choice—to ensure that they have a positive and successful learning experience that embraces both their identity and their desire to earn degrees in STEM, or to continue as is, with significant numbers of Blacks dropping out of the STEM fields due to racism and an unequal system of education that calls into question their intellect and potential for success. Colleges and universities nearly every day claim to promote diversity. Both the public and the private sector send messages that we need more diversity in STEM in order to be globally competitive and to fill STEM-related positions in the United States. Yet most colleges and universities haven't changed the rules of the game—they often operate using the same approach that maintains the status quo, White and male. If higher education is serious about being more inclusive, it must have deep and critical conversations about what needs to be changed. These changes will need to address core assumptions about race and racism in society and how these shape and direct our policies and practices, including the way STEM courses are taught and students are supported, the biases held by faculty and students, the intense focus on competition, the obsession with supporting only the "best" students, and the insincerity of "efforts" to achieve faculty diversity. Doing otherwise shows a lack of commitment to diversity overall.

We here issue a plea to all colleges and universities to rethink their STEM education, to question the racial biases embedded in popular teaching practices, and to take institutional responsibility for the success of African American students. We offer an agenda for promoting greater racial equity by considering practices that can alter the rules of the game, leading to wider access to the opportunities that facilitate achievement in STEM for Black students. These practices are drawn from what we learned at the ten HBCUs discussed in this book. Many HBCUs have been using these practices for decades and have disproportionately positive results for African Americans in STEM, given their size and resources and the preparation of many of their students. Rather than assuming they have all the answers, colleges and universities across the nation would benefit from looking to HBCUs for expertise in STEM education. Our agenda below offers a primer for making change. The next step is to engage these practices and these institutions for guidance in STEM success for all students.

An Agenda for Diversity in Twenty-First-Century STEM Fields

Take Responsibility

Enacting institutional responsibility to promote Black student achievement in STEM is rooted in the very belief that all students have the inherent intelligence and capacity to learn and succeed, no matter their circumstances. Our colleges and universities must promote a belief that all students can succeed, and must take responsibility to ensure that success. Institutional responsibility involves understanding the circumstances that can limit student progress and taking action to mitigate their influence—in essence, centering and privileging students who need greater attention and support. Campus leaders must focus on addressing differences in learning gaps among students of various racial and ethnic backgrounds. Rather than merely pointing fingers at students for their lack of performance, we must consider the institution's responsibility to carry these students forward.

Focus on Inclusivity

Instead of focusing on being more exclusive and elite, which has become a national obsession among many colleges and universities, we must pride ourselves on becoming more inclusive and being responsible for student success.[2] These messages of inclusivity and success must also come from presidents of colleges and universities, replacing the messages that reinforce exclusion and racial prejudices on many campuses. Promoting a truly inclusive campus requires institutions to acknowledge and dismantle the very practices (e.g., language and how the narrative of STEM is constructed on campus) and policies (e.g., course prerequisites based on narrow definitions of college readiness) that sort students out of STEM. Colleges and universities must ask themselves what would happen if they stopped focusing on only the "best" students and took seriously the education of all their students—adding value to these students more fully, as higher education was intended to do.

See Inherent Success

Improving students' chances of success in STEM starts and stops with faculty members believing that students can, in fact, achieve. This cannot occur unless faculty members see inherent promise in all students. Among HBCUs, one of the approaches to ensuring that students see themselves as successful is to introduce them to former students—even those who struggled—who are now successful alumni serving in medicine, industry, and academe across the nation, bringing them back to campus not only at the beginning of the academic year but throughout students' academic programs. Students are particularly motivated by those alumni who faced challenges and know the ways to overcome them. Faculty members must condition students to believe in their success and their ability to learn, because so much of their future accomplishments will be tied to how well they build the internal capacity to persevere in the face of increased challenges.

Understand Students' Full Lives

When faculty members dedicate time to engaging with students and understanding the relationships between their lives and their potential for success in college, they can guide their colleges and universities in beginning to construct the pathway to success for underrepresented and often disadvantaged students. Rather than seeing all students in STEM as the same, faculty members must take the time to learn students' names and associate their names with their talents, and to learn their stories and remember what motivates them to succeed in the classroom. If classes are too large to do so, it is imperative that teaching assistants spend time doing this work so that students feel included, noticed, and respected in their learning process. Faculty members need to realize that students do not leave behind their families and communities when they become students; they do not detach from their former lives. Learning to navigate the various relationships and obligations in their lives is essential to how well students walk their pathway to a degree. Faculty members and staff can proactively assist students by providing them with, or connecting them to, resources on campus so that students can more effectively meet their academic obligations. If faculty members are at all interested in the success of their students, they must embrace the reality that the traditional responsibilities of faculty—teaching, advising, and research—must begin to evolve to meet the needs of an increasingly diverse student population.

Realize That Success Is Not an Aberration

Faculty members and administrators should refrain from seeing success and achievement as belonging to a minority of students. Rather than focus on success aberrations—those students who stand out above everyone else in classrooms and careers—colleges and universities need to concentrate on those students who are making significant gains in the classroom, given their pre-college preparation and background. Success aberrations are typically highly successful before they enter college and need little assistance. If faculty members focus on students who have the desire and drive but need additional training and nurturing, achievement could become the norm rather than the exception. When faculty members acknowledge this simple distinction between these two types of students, they are taking a crucial step in reshaping how they work with and provide students with the opportunities they need to thrive in STEM.

Assume That Students Need Your Help to Do Well

Faculty members must be proactive about approaching students rather than merely reactive to the needs they openly express. Students are often left on their own to "persevere," with faculty members not paying them much attention. Telling students to "stay strong," to "keep working hard," is an empty message unless it is paired with evidence that they are welcomed and included in the STEM community. Students need to know that even though an institution might not have been built for them at the time of its construction, it is being renovated to include them. Being proactively supportive means anticipating challenges and stepping up before students are in danger of faltering, and expanding the role and training of faculty members so that they are equipped to engage students as whole people.

Give Students Daily Exposure to STEM Curricula

To be successful in STEM, students need daily exposure and daily exercise. Learning in the STEM fields is cumulative. Many students interested in excelling in STEM fields do not come from math-rich backgrounds, and for them to be brought up to speed and learn the foundational elements for STEM courses, they need daily exposure to the material. A lack of preparation does not mean students cannot excel in STEM; it means that they need more exposure to sound study skills

and opportunities to work with the material to reach their goals—and
it is the job of faculty members to provide these opportunities. Just as
we build muscle in the body to become stronger physically, students
must build their muscles in STEM to ensure their success. It is essential that faculty members begin to consider intelligence as malleable—
like a muscle that grows with hard work—as opposed to estimating a
person's intelligence in terms of their current shortcomings or their
lack of opportunities in life. Faculty members must dig deeper to find
the true talent in students, using all their skills to provoke learning.
The messages that students receive about their intelligence matter—
they can motivate or they can deter.

Privilege Collaboration over Competition

Within most colleges and universities, individualism is privileged over
collaboration and community; faculty members often tell students that
many of them will crack under the pressure and challenges of the
courses, suggesting that not all students are meant for STEM degrees.[3]
However, our HBCUs teach us how both faculty members and students
can collaborate to have a richer experience. Students, working collaboratively to solve problems and challenges, realize that they all make
more significant progress when they support each other and work as a
team. They understand that none of them lose out by helping others,
and that in fact they benefit greatly from the knowledge and support
of their peers. Students see other students as part of the learning process and integral to their success when faculty members discourage
solitariness and competition.

And faculty members at these HBCUs—who work together across
disciplines, classes, and curricula—learn that they benefit from a more
welcoming and family-like environment in which their regular

communication with each other strengthens the work they do for and with students. Those faculty members who emphasize collaboration, and maintain communication with each other, contribute to an optimal learning environment for students. Students benefit from consistency and a wider network of support across faculty members. Of most importance, faculty members who support one another normalize and model a culture of community that pushes against the culture of competition that permeated most STEM programs.

Collect and Share Data on and with Students

The colleges and universities that experience significant success with their students are typically those that know their students well and regularly measure their progress.[4] Students perform better when faculty members and academic staff know where they are likely to falter. They also do better when data pertaining to their performance are regularly collected and shared with them—no one critical to the achievement of students is left out of the support process. Operating in the dark does students a disservice. Faculty and staff must come together to understand the data and to coordinate their time and resources to address areas, such as curriculum and academic services, that are hindering students' progress.

Reward Teaching in Faculty Evaluation Systems

When the reward systems for faculty members neglect teaching, colleges and universities neglect students. Reward systems that push teaching and speak to students' needs result in student-centered teaching and more cooperation among faculty members in their efforts to teach. Because faculty members create the reward systems within colleges and universities, they have the power to change it. They also have an obligation to be familiar with what kind of teaching techniques lead to enhanced student learning. Faculty often do not have the will to make these changes, or to emphasize teaching, because their research is what propels them to success in the academy. However, with changes in the reward system across institutions, it is possible to even out the emphasis on teaching and research. One of the reasons faculty members do not spend time on teaching, and do not put students' needs first, is that most reward systems for faculty members do not put students first.

In research universities, it is expected that the reward, tenure, and promotion processes will reward research. Teaching is mostly an afterthought. More comprehensive universities, which tend to be state schools or regionally focused, have been increasingly emphasizing research in an effort to keep up with the major research institutions in their states. And even small liberal arts colleges, which have emphasized teaching for decades, have increased their demand that faculty conduct and publish research. We recognize that altering the reward structure speaks to much larger issues that are well beyond the scope of this book, and we do recognize the value of research, but we also believe that the well-being of our students, especially those most vulnerable in society, warrants greater and continued conversation around how this structure should change.

Link STEM Education to Societal Justice

Faculty members at each of the HBCUs we visited talked about their commitment to students being rooted in their school's mission and commitment to social justice. They see the success of African American students in STEM as a social justice issue due to the vast inequities across the STEM and health-care industries, as well as academia. They also see HBCUs as a mechanism for producing scholars who are dedicated to promoting a just and humane society. Faculty members are less focused on graduation and more focused on where students end up once they graduate. The social justice mentality of HBCU faculty members results in a focus on students' learning needs. What we found in STEM departments at HBCUs resonates with college and university rankings in the *Washington Monthly*, which, unlike the *U.S. News & World Report* rankings, focus on institutions that add value to students and have a focus on social justice and service.[5]

A focus on minority achievement in STEM education is often couched within a broader narrative of strengthening the U.S. economy. For us, the need to increase Black and other minority representation in STEM education and occupations is a matter of racial equity *and* the opportunity for upward social mobility. According to the latest data from the Center on Education and the Workforce, STEM occupations are not only some of the highest paid at each level of education but also some of the fastest-growing, "By 2018, the share of STEM occupations in the economy will grow to 5 percent, up from 4.4 percent in 2005—a growth in the number of STEM jobs from 6.8 million in 2008 to 8 million by 2018."[6] We want Black and other minority students to take advantage of these opportunities, not only to improve their financial standing and the lives of their families and communities, but so that they are in position to influence and contribute to a brighter and more equitable vision of society.

View Students as Family

Viewing students as family at HBCUs has nothing to do with "students' immaturity" or "coddling." Instead, it refers to the amount of energy and resources faculty members are willing to deploy for their students. As students at the HBCUs in this study were viewed as family, faculty members were protective and held them accountable on a daily basis. The very notion of family means offering unwavering support while having high expectations. The combination of the two leads to success for students who want to be both held accountable and nurtured in their learning environments.

With this agenda, which draws from decades of practice taking place at the HBCUs featured in this book, we hope that readers will push back on status quo practices in STEM classrooms and programs across the nation. Moreover, we hope that STEM faculty members and practitioners will have the will to provide the best learning experiences for African American students and all students.

Concluding Thoughts

OUR REASON FOR BEGINNING this research was to help colleges and universities address the grave underrepresentation of Black students in the STEM fields and the STEM workforce. Racial inequality is one of our nation's greatest challenges, and cannot be significantly addressed without improving how our schools and universities provide meaningful opportunities for Black and other minority students to fully realize their potential. We draw our solutions and inspiration for addressing racial inequality in education from the very institutions—HBCUs—built to teach and nurture children of Black communities when no other college would; these institutions are, in fact, disproportionately succeeding at graduating Blacks in STEM disciplines.

We have shared with you what we believe makes these HBCUs successful. We hope that we have convinced you that the changes we have recommended begin with a shift in institutional and individual will and perception about students' capacity to succeed. But more than that, we wanted to share the voices and experiences of African American students so that PWIs and other colleges and universities may draw inspiration to develop and advance new and different approaches to meeting the needs of African Americans in STEM programs. These HBCUs provide ample evidence that it is partly our fault—the fault of faculty, staff, and even university presidents—when our African American students do not succeed. If we truly care about their success, their ability to make a difference, armed with a degree in STEM, we will reinvigorate and reconfigure our institutions so that our faculties' composition, classrooms, and labs become more inclusive domains of scholarship and opportunity.

Of course, we would be remiss to assume that higher education alone can address what W. E. B. Du Bois considered "the problem of the color line."[1] The quality of education—how it functions, and who it *best* serves—is partly shaped by our economy, industries, and industry leaders. They dictate what type of discipline is valued, how it should be taught, and who benefits from mastering its concepts.[2] Although this book is a call to action for colleges and universities to reconsider their practices in teaching and promoting achievement in STEM, it is equally relevant to the very corporations that hire our college graduates. Colleges and universities are sensitive to shifts and trends in the workforce because they wish to see their graduates successfully translate their hard-earned degrees into full-time opportunities. Therefore, we urge businesses, nonprofit organizations, and government agencies and offices that depend on and value STEM-educated individuals to use their influence to demand better from our institutions of higher learning. If they do not, they too are equally at fault.

To our student readers, especially students like Jesse, who have been penalized by the system because of the color of their skin or their cultural background, this book is also about and written for you. Right now, you may be deciding to pursue a career in STEM or in a health field, or perhaps you are already knee-deep into your upper-division classes. We hope that you take from this book an understanding that colleges and universities have an obligation to see you through on your chosen pathway. This is not to suggest that you, yourself, can't make personal choices that have negative consequences. But the general struggles you will face in STEM fields are not outcomes of your own actions. Your potential struggles in STEM are an outcome of a society that is structured to limit the quality of your choices and opportunities to succeed. Throughout this book, we have discussed how some colleges and universities reinforce beliefs and practices that discourage the achievement of Black students, and we have demonstrated how changes to the environment and pedagogy—as inspired by the HBCUs in this book—can help reverse that trend. As you move forward in your education and in life, we hope that our research informs you to seek institutions and communities that are actively and deeply committed to your realizing your best self. Vet the institutions carefully. Gather information on curriculum and teaching styles. Meet with faculty members and ask them the tough questions, including their perceptions and approaches to achievement in STEM. You owe it to yourself to receive an education from an institution that will embrace all that you are and all that you can become.

Eliminating racial inequality is not the responsibility of Black communities, especially HBCUs. But they can serve as an inspiration if we allow ourselves the possibility of change that requires a deep look at our core values and beliefs.

APPENDIX

NOTES

ACKNOWLEDGMENTS

INDEX

APPENDIX

The Study

We selected ten (10) HBCUs to participate in our study through a competitive process based on having one or more models of success related to STEM education, paying specific attention to gateway courses, which often have a detrimental impact on African American student success. The competitive process involved a national call for proposals, inviting all four-year HBCUs to submit proposals. We based the selection of the participating HBCUs on a simple, straightforward proposal (two pages) and budget (one page) that highlighted the institution's best practices in STEM and crafted a new capacity-building project related to enhancing learning in STEM education. Based upon input from a national advisory board of STEM professionals and experts, we selected the following institutions to participate in the study, which was called HBCUs as Leaders in STEM: Claflin University (SC), North Carolina

Central University (NC), Lincoln University (PA), Cheyney University (PA), Morgan State University (MD), Delaware State University (DE), Xavier University of Louisiana (LA), Dillard University (LA), Prairie View A&M University (TX), and Huston-Tillotson University (TX).

To ensure diversity among the HBCUs, we took the following into consideration: public or private status; geographical region; religious affiliation; institutional size; and their national reputation in STEM. Once we selected the institutions, we visited the respective colleges and universities and, in collaboration with institutional representatives, we studied and highlighted models of success that illuminated those characteristics of HBCUs that exemplify powerful strategies for success in STEM education. For the purpose of this study, STEM includes the biological and agricultural sciences, engineering, mathematics, statistics, computer science, and the physical sciences. Engaging faculty members, staff, and students in the process, we explored instructional approaches to gateway courses and pathways to STEM degrees, incentives and rewards for good teaching in STEM, and non-instructional support systems that foster student learning and achievement. Through this qualitative study, we collected data through observations, individual and focus group interviews, and document analysis. We also analyzed quantitative data provided by the individual institutions, as well as data available through the National Science Foundation, to form our protocols and contextualize our findings. It is important to note that we gave all individuals interviewed for this research project pseudonyms, with the exception of the ten HBCU presidents, as it would have been impossible to mask these individuals. We gave faculty and staff full names upon first use and then a last name, and students first names only.

We also allotted funds to each participating institution to launch a data-driven intervention pertaining to STEM education on their campus. These capacity-building grants, along with the overarching grant, were focused on helping HBCUs elevate themselves, their student success, and their faculty members' talent as leaders in STEM. We used this collaborative approach to the research process to mirror the collaboration exemplified by HBCUs and to be more egalitarian in our research efforts. Of note, most of the HBCUs created new STEM programs with their funding. However, a few supplemented programs that already existed and strengthened them. The funds also were spent to support supplemental instructors, students in summer bridge programs, student attendance at STEM conferences, faculty summer salaries to lead summer bridge programs, and faculty travel when co-presenting with students at academic conferences. Although many PWIs have ample funding to send students and faculty members to conferences and to pay for supplemental instructors, most HBCUs do not have large enough budgets to fund those.

One of our goals for this research project was to provide national exposure to the work being conducted at HBCUs—work that results in disproportionate success for African Americans in the STEM fields. To garner national exposure, we published a major report and hosted a national convening in which all the HBCU partners presented their success models and highlighted their capacity-building projects before an audience that included scholars, media, funders, students, policymakers, and nonprofit leaders. In addition, we pitched stories to media outlets, resulting in articles about the effective work at many of our participating institutions in the *New York Times*, the *Washington Post*, the *Chronicle of Higher Education, Diverse Issues*, and the Associated Press, and on National Public Radio.

Although this book is focused more broadly on STEM and fostering success in STEM across colleges and universities than it is on HBCUs, it is important for the reader to understand the context of each of the HBCUs from which we are drawing successful strategies to propel African American students to success in the STEM fields. The following descriptions provide context on the ten HBCUs. See Table 1.

Table 1. Historically Black Colleges and Universities Featured in This Study

Institution	Location	Total Enrollment	High School GPA	Average Combined SAT Score	% of First-Year Students Receiving Pell Grant
Dillard University	New Orleans, LA	1,200	2.92	860	78
Xavier University of Louisiana	New Orleans, LA	2,976	3.37	985	57
Prairie View A&M University	Prairie View, TX	8,429	3.10	845	78
North Carolina Central University	Durham, NC	7,687	3.10	860	79
Delaware State University	Dover, DE	4,397	2.80	895	53
Morgan State University	Baltimore, MD	7,689	3.00	900	75
Claflin University	Orangeburg, SC	1,866	3.28	880	89
Lincoln University	Oxford, PA	2,000	3.00	855	66
Cheyney University	Cheyney, PA	1,022	2.50	n/a	77
Huston-Tillotson University	Austin, TX	1,031	2.79	800	74

Source: The College Navigator, National Center for Educational Statistics, 2018.

DILLARD UNIVERSITY, NEW ORLEANS, LOUISIANA

Dillard University's mission is to create graduates who become world leaders who are broadly educated, culturally aware, and concerned with improving the human condition by using a highly personalized and student-centered approach. The university, which is situated on beautiful grounds boasting green grass, wispy trees, and white buildings, has a total enrollment of 1,200. The average high school GPA among first-year students is 2.92 and the average SAT math and verbal combined score is 860. A full 78 percent of Dillard's first-year students receive Pell grants, indicating the high percentage of low-income students at the university. When we visited the campus, we noticed that most STEM majors were first-generation college students who had little exposure to formal STEM programs or role models in STEM prior to attending Dillard. However, they had a love of math and science and a willingness to push themselves hard to succeed. They were also eager to take advantage of opportunities placed in front of them, because they knew that they would be supported even if they stumbled.

For the purposes of our research, we examined three programs at Dillard. In the Systemic Mentoring Program (SMP), faculty members are paired with students interested in STEM fields and students are awarded stipends that support their research. Peer Assisted Study Sessions (PASS) assist students majoring in STEM programs with courses that are paramount to their academic success. Also highlighted is the Research Experience for Undergraduates (REU), which gives support to six students for research projects completed during the summer months. Students are given a stipend, which includes on-campus housing for room and board.

XAVIER UNIVERSITY OF LOUISIANA, NEW ORLEANS, LOUISIANA

Xavier University of Louisiana is the only HBCU affiliated with the Roman Catholic Church in the United States. Xavier contributes to the promotion of a more just and humane society by preparing its students to assume roles of leadership and service in a global society. The university's diverse learning and teaching environment incorporates research and community service throughout the curriculum. Xavier University has a total enrollment of 2,976. Its first-year students have an average high school GPA of 3.37 and an average SAT combined math and verbal score of 985. Over 57 percent of the institution's first-year students are Pell Grant recipients.

During our visit, we were struck by the generations of families that had attended Xavier for their education. Students told us of aunts, uncles, parents, even grandparents who had attended the school and recommended it. Different from many of the HBCUs in our research, Xavier has larger numbers of second-generation college students from middle-class families, but it still enrolls many low-income and first-generation students. Yet in the STEM fields, the largest percentage of students had college-educated parents or close relatives who had earned college degrees. Moreover, many of the students have various individuals in their families with STEM backgrounds. Students were also fully aware that attending Xavier meant that they were smart and committed and would succeed in their given area. Communities in the New Orleans area were constantly given this message.

Considered a leader in the STEM community, Xavier has two programs profiled in this research project: its peer- and instructor-led drill system, and its peer-led student tutoring centers. Both programs were developed for students enrolled in general and organic chemistry—courses that tend to have high attrition of Black students. The peer- and instructor-led drill system monitors student progress and provides constant reinforcement of concepts and skills, with two-hour drill classes once per week. Peer-led tutoring is an institutionalized practice at Xavier. Selected by faculty members, peer tutors are available throughout the day at centers on campus, ensuring that students have ample access to support.

PRAIRIE VIEW A&M UNIVERSITY, PRAIRIE VIEW, TEXAS

Prairie View A&M University is the second-oldest public institution of higher learning in Texas. The university has been recognized for its reputation of producing engineers, nurses, and educators. A member of the Texas A&M University system, the university is dedicated to fulfilling its land-grant mission of achieving distinction in teaching, research, and service. Prairie View A&M University is home to the International Goat Research Center, which was established in 1981 and conducts research "in the areas of genetics, reproductive physiology, nutrition and veterinary health."[1] Prairie View A&M University has an enrollment of 8,429 students. Its first-year students have an average high school GPA of 3.10 and an average SAT combined math and verbal score of 845. Of the first-year students, 78 percent are recipients of Pell Grants.

During our visit to campus, we met families of students spanning several generations that had been taught by the faculty members at Prairie View, as well as students who were the first in their family to attend college. They chose to attend Prairie View for its reputation for sending students to medical school and other health professions. Students learned, from brothers and sisters as well as parents, of the institution and its track record in STEM and even specific faculty member's success with students. Like Xavier students, many of the Prairie View students in STEM were from middle-class families and had college-educated parents. Of note, those students in the premedical program, in particular, were much more likely to come from college-educated parents and to have had considerable exposure to STEM curricula and STEM role models. They regularly shared stories about members of their families who promised they would find success at Prairie View should they decide to attend.

Prairie View A&M University's Department of Biology has created two successful programs to improve the achievement and retention of their students in the STEM fields. Premedical Concepts Institute (PCI) is a rigorous ten-week summer program for incoming freshmen who are interested in pursuing STEM careers. The Cardiovascular and Microbial Research Center provides undergraduate students with research projects and mentoring that support independent problem solving. Both programs are meant to promote engagement in STEM and, in turn, facilitate degree attainment and aspiration for advanced or professional studies.

NORTH CAROLINA CENTRAL UNIVERSITY, DURHAM, NORTH CAROLINA

North Carolina Central University was established as the first public liberal arts institution of higher learning for African Americans in the United States. Located in Durham, the university advances research in various subjects, including the biotechnological, biomedical, informational, and computational sciences, history, legal education, and the behavioral, social, and health sciences. North Carolina Central University has an enrollment of 7,687 students. First-year students' average high school GPA is 3.1, and their average combined SAT math and verbal score is 860. Over 79 percent of first-year students are Pell Grants recipients.

During our visit, we noticed that students were well-rounded and enthusiastic about earning STEM degrees, but also somewhat unsure about their own skills. Unlike Xavier University or Prairie View, the students at North Carolina Central University were less likely to have parents who attended college or exposure to STEM role models. They were, however, very close to faculty members and shared that their uncertainty was buffered by faculty members' belief in their abilities to succeed. Students were also energized by the new chancellor at the time, who envisioned a future where North Carolina Central was at the nexus of technology and innovation.[2] Located in the heart of the Research Triangle, North Carolina Central University is in a good position for this.

APPENDIX

As part of this research project, we profiled the Peer Mentoring and Technology (PMT) program in the Departments of Biology and Mathematics and Physics as a model for enhancing persistence and success. PMT provides a research-based understanding for freshmen majoring in science and mathematics. Students participate in peer-led teaching and learning (PLTL) activities that are an important aspect of courses for the students. PLTL is considered a high-impact practice that is primarily a supplement to large enrollment classes. It ensures that students are engaged and learning the overall principles of their coursework.

DELAWARE STATE UNIVERSITY, DOVER, DELAWARE

Since 1957, Delaware State University has been a hub for teaching, research, and public service in the Dover region. Delaware State serves a diverse student population and has an enrollment of 4,397. The institution's first-year students have an average high school GPA of 2.8 and an average combined SAT math and verbal score of 895. Nearly 53 percent of Delaware State's first-year students are Pell Grant recipients.

During our visit, we met with students from all types of backgrounds. Some were full-time students; others were part-time commuters, working full-time and striving to change their lives by earning a degree in STEM. Many of the students were older than those at the other HBCUs we visited and were juggling many family responsibilities. Nevertheless, they were firmly committed to pursuing degrees in STEM and benefited from the family-like environment at the university.

Delaware State offers two effective programs profiled in this study: The Science and Math Initiative for Learning Enrichment (SMILE) Project and the Mathematics Preparation Program (MP2). The SMILE Project is a year-long STEM learning community, which includes an online summer developmental math course, a STEM training camp, peer mentoring, a mathematics workshop, and an undergraduate research program. The SMILE Project also sponsors peer mentors and leaders and offers students the opportunity to participate in undergraduate research. MP2 is an enrichment program that prepares high school students and pre-freshmen for college-level coursework through summer courses in mathematics and English.

MORGAN STATE UNIVERSITY, BALTIMORE, MARYLAND

Morgan State University is the leading public urban research university in Maryland, known for its quality in teaching, intensive research, successful public service, and community engagement. The campus is in the heart of Baltimore and highly engaged with the local community. Morgan State University has an enrollment of 7,689 students. The institution's first-year students have an average high school GPA of 3.0 and an average combined SAT math and verbal score of 900. Over 75 percent of Morgan State's first-year students are Pell Grant recipients.

When we were on campus, we noticed a high level of interaction, camaraderie, and laughing among STEM students—they talked of the close friendships and necessity of these friendships to succeed in STEM at Morgan State. Students regularly pushed each other to succeed and saw how intertwined their actions or lack of actions were in relation to their overall success at the institution.[3] These talks of collaboration, friendship, and academic success were, however, foregrounded by the immense racial strife and unrest across Baltimore that occurred right before our visit. These students' remarks about achievement revealed their inherent desires to improve the well-being of their communities.

Within the School of Computer, Mathematical and Natural Sciences, Morgan State has developed the Foundations of Mathematics (FOM) summer program for incoming freshmen engineering students. The five-week course is an online and in-person workshop that meets on Saturdays for four hours.

Students work independently online during the week and in teams on Saturdays with juniors and seniors for coaches / tutors. The program uses Assessment and Learning in Knowledge Spaces (ALEKS) auto-adaptive mathematics software for instruction.

CLAFLIN UNIVERSITY, ORANGEBURG, SOUTH CAROLINA

Claflin University is a small private liberal arts college affiliated with the United Methodist Church. The university enrolls 1,866 students. First-year students have an average high school GPA of 3.28 and an average combined SAT math and verbal score 880. A full 89 percent of first-year students are Pell Grant recipients.

At Claflin University, we learned that most of the students were from very poor families, were first-generation college students, and had little exposure to STEM role models before attending Claflin. Located in rural South Carolina, away from any large nearby cities, and in the impoverished "corridor of shame," the institution has an excellent record in STEM and for placing students into selective graduate programs and corporate opportunities.[4]

As part of the Pre-Freshman Year Summer Program, incoming freshmen take rigorous courses in math and chemistry. The students have a student tutor who lives, studies, and eats with them to help them foster and strengthen their interests and skills in STEM. Student tutors are juniors and seniors who receive specialized training from Claflin faculty members. Claflin also provides Supplemental Instruction (SI), which affords increased support and tutoring for students in STEM gateway courses.

LINCOLN UNIVERSITY, OXFORD, PENNSYLVANIA

Lincoln University was founded in 1854 and is located 45 miles southwest of Philadelphia in Oxford, Pennsylvania. The campus is surrounded by mushroom farms, wineries, and gorgeous landscapes. Lincoln serves approximately 1,600 undergraduate students and 400 graduate students. More than 90 percent of Lincoln students are African American. As one of the country's first degree-granting historically Black institutions, Lincoln has been a key component in educating African Americans in the region, especially students coming from nearby Delaware and the urban areas of Philadelphia and Chester. Lincoln University first-year students have an average high school GPA of 3.0 and an average combined SAT math and verbal score of 855. Nearly 66 percent of first-year students receive Pell Grants.

When we visited, we noticed that the students had a keen intensity about pursuing their STEM degrees. They were closely mentored, their lives were steeped in research and lab experiences, and they were focused on their future success. Students benefit from having relatively new and elaborate facilities on campus, which is not the norm on most under-resourced campuses, including HBCUs.

Lincoln has several programs that have succeeded in improving STEM achievement. As part of this research project, Lincoln's Excellent Academic Program in Science (LEAPS) and its Supplemental Instruction (SI) program to retain and graduate students majoring in STEM were profiled. LEAPS is a six-week summer bridge program to support incoming freshmen through their transition to college STEM programs. SI provides additional tutoring for students in STEM gateway courses.

CHEYNEY UNIVERSITY, CHEYNEY, PENNSYLVANIA

Founded in 1837 as the Institute for Colored Youth, Cheyney University of Pennsylvania is the first institution of higher learning for African Americans in the United States. Cheyney offers bachelor's degrees in more than thirty disciplines and a master's degree in education. The University enrolls 1,022 students. The average high school GPA among first-year students is 2.50. The institution does not require SAT scores. Over 77 percent of Cheyney's first-year students receive Pell Grants.

Although Cheyney University has endured difficult times as of late, its STEM programs remain strong. Students we met with were determined to succeed in STEM and were goal-oriented, but they had had little exposure to STEM role models in their families or lives. Most were from low-income families in which few people had attended college. Students relied on faculty members to motivate them toward success and to support them when their safety nets no longer held. Of note, most of the students we talked to at Cheyney were working several jobs or working full-time while attending college full-time, making academic work even more challenging.

Two programs that are helping students in STEM at Cheyney University are The Coach Approach and the Aquaculture / Aquaponics research program. The Coach Approach is an intense method of mentoring in which support for learning, research experience, and plans are closely tailored to the individual student. Faculty members and students are paired together from start to finish, and faculty members provide continuous academic and professional advice, presenting and publishing research, and emotional support during students' tenure. The Aquaculture / Aquaponics research program includes the Aquaculture Research and Education Laboratory, which provides students with real-world industry experience. Students are exposed to the research and business development sides of the scientific community.

HUSTON–TILLOTSON UNIVERSITY, AUSTIN, TEXAS

Huston-Tillotson is a private four-year institution. It provides educational opportunity with an emphasis on academic excellence, spiritual and ethical development, civic engagement, and leadership to a diverse population of students. Huston-Tillotson University enrolls 1,031 students. The average high school GPA for its first-year students is 2.79, and their average combined SAT math and verbal score is 800. Of the first-year students, 74 percent receive Pell Grants.

Huston-Tillotson is located in East Austin in an area of the city that has traditionally been home to African Americans due to the Jim Crow laws that segregated the city earlier in its history. Most of the students come from the local area and various surrounding areas, and include a mix of African American and Latino students. As the only HBCU in the growing state capital of Texas, Huston-Tillotson joins a rich community of postsecondary institutions, including the University of Texas–Austin, Texas State University, and Austin Community College.

As part of this research, Huston-Tillotson has an Integrative Teaching and Learning program and a Reading Comprehension program to increase the quality of preparation for students in STEM. Faculty members also participate in professional development opportunities throughout the academic year and in the summer. The initiative seeks to strengthen the ability of students studying STEM fields by incorporating cross-disciplinary material into key courses in the general education requirements.

Each of these ten HBCUs offers a unique approach while also drawing on the history and culture of HBCUs overall—a history and culture that are focused on uplifting African Americans and that can serve as the impetus for other colleges and universities to better serve their students. To achieve the goal of this book, we draw inspiration from all ten HBCUs and selectively discuss practices from each campus that best illustrate the points we wish to make.

We think it is important to reiterate that this study is qualitative in scope, with a goal of capturing narratives and expressions—which are often difficult to present quantitatively—of practices at these ten HBCUs in order to help reveal a culture of success for their students. We conducted large-scale, deep-dive case studies of the ten HBCUs. Our findings pertain to these ten schools. Although much can be learned from our findings about HBCU culture and potential for success in STEM, we want to be clear that our research is not representative of all HBCUs in STEM, nor can it be automatically applied to majority colleges and universities. However, we do think that our findings can provoke change, foster new approaches, provide opportunity for thoughtful reflections across STEM departments at all types of institutions, and serve as an impetus for increased focus on student success overall.

Lastly, although this book is based on a rigorous three-year academic research project, we have not written in an academic tone. We purposefully, and with the encouragement and blessing of our editor at Harvard University Press, wrote *Making Black Scientists* for a more general audience. Although there is ample scholarship to back up our claims, and our data provides grounding for our findings, our book is written to be accessible to anyone who picks it up to read—from a high school student interested in STEM, to a parent interested in helping their child find the best STEM program, to the STEM college professor interested in providing a more supportive learning environment, to the scholar conducting research. Our aim is to push those interested and working in the STEM fields to reconsider approaches to learning, firmly root students at the center of learning, and be open to the lessons that HBCUs can teach all of us about fostering success in STEM.

NOTES

INTRODUCTION

1. We use the terms "Black" and "African American" interchangeably in this book. All African Americans are, in fact, also Black. We are, however, not talking about Blacks from the Caribbean or Africa when we refer to Blacks in this manuscript or in any of the data presented. We chose to use "Black" and "African American" as interchangeable because those we interviewed identified as so throughout our discussions.

2. Nicole M. Stephens, Stephanie A. Fryberg, Hazel Rose Markus, Camille S. Johnson, and Rebecca Covarrubias, "Unseen Disadvantage: How American Universities' Focus on Independence Undermines the Academic Performance of First-Generation College Students," *Journal of Personality and Social Psychology* 102, no. 6 (2012): 1178.

3. Yu Xie, Michael Fang, and Kimberlee Shauman, "STEM Education," *Annual Review of Sociology* 41 (2015): 331–357.

4. James D. Anderson, *The Education of Blacks in the South, 1865–1930* (Chapel Hill: University of North Carolina Press, 1988); Gary Orfield, Patricia Marin, and Catherine Horn, *Higher Education and the Color Line: College Access, Racial Equity, and Social Change* (Cambridge, MA: Harvard Education Press, 2005).

5. Craig Steven Wilder, *Ebony and Ivy: Race, Slavery, and the Troubled History of America's Universities* (New York: Bloomsbury, 2014); Peter Sacks, "How Colleges Perpetuate Inequality," *Chronicle of Higher Education,* January 12, 2007.

6. Robert Teranishi, Walter R. Allen, and Daniel G. Solorzano, "Opportunity at the Crossroads: Racial Inequality, School Segregation, and Higher Education in California," *Teachers College Record* 106, no. 11 (2004): 2224–2245; Estela Mara Bensimon, "Closing the Achievement Gap in Higher Education: An Organizational Learning Perspective," *New Directions for Higher Education*131 (2005): 99; Eduardo Bonilla-Silva, *Racism without Racists: Color-Blind Racism and the Persistence of Racial Inequality in America* (Lanham, MD: Rowman and Littlefield, 2017); Mitchell L. Stevens, Elizabeth A. Armstrong, and Richard Arum, "Sieve, Incubator, Temple, Hub: Empirical and Theoretical Advances in the Sociology of Higher Education," *Annual Review of Sociology* 34 (2008): 127–151.

7. Orfield, Marin, and Horn, *Higher Education.*

8. John R. Thelin, *A History of American Higher Education* (Baltimore: Johns Hopkins University Press, 2011).

9. Anderson, *Education of Blacks;* W. E. B. Du Bois, *Black Reconstruction in America: Toward a History of the Part Which Black Folk Played in the Attempt to Reconstruct Democracy in America, 1860–1880* (New Brunswick, NJ: Transaction, 2013).

10. There were three HBCUs in the North prior to the end of the Civil War: Cheyney University (Pennsylvania), Lincoln University (Pennsylvania), and Wilberforce University (Ohio). Each university was created by abolitionist missionaries.

11. Anderson, *Education of Blacks*; Thelin, *History of American Higher Education*.

12. William Boland and Marybeth Gasman, "America's Public HBCUs: A Four State Comparison of Institutional Capacity and State Funding Priorities," Penn Center for Minority Serving Institutions, 2014, https://cmsi.gse.upenn.edu/sites/default/files/four_state_comparison.pdf; William Casey Boland, "The Impact of Performance-Based Funding on Historically Black Colleges and Universities," in *Administrative Challenges and Organizational Leadership in Historically Black Colleges and Universities*, ed. Charles Prince and Rochelle Ford (New York: IGI Global, 2016), 151; Marybeth Gasman, Andrés Castro Samayoa, William C. Boland, Amanda Washington, and Chris D. Jimenez, "Investing in Student Success: The Return on Investment for Minority Serving Institutions," Penn Center for Minority Serving Institutions, 2015, https://cmsi.gse.upenn.edu/sites/default/files/MSI_ROIreport_R6.pdf.

13. Boland and Gasman, "America's Public HBCUs"; Boland, "Impact of Performance-Based Funding"; Robert Palmer, Ryan Davis, and Marybeth Gasman, "A Matter of Diversity, Equity, and Necessity: The Tension between Maryland's Higher Education System and Its Historically Black Colleges and Universities over the Office of Civil Rights Agreement," *Journal of Negro Education* 80, no. 2 (2011): 121–133.

14. Michelle Alexander, *The New Jim Crow: Mass Incarceration in the Age of Colorblindness* (New York: New Press, 2012).

15. Marybeth Gasman, *Envisioning Black Colleges: A History of the United Negro College Fund* (Baltimore: Johns Hopkins University Press, 2007).

16. Aldon Morris, *The Scholar Denied: W. E. B. Du Bois and the Birth of Modern Sociology* (Berkeley: University of California Press, 2015); W. E. B.

Du Bois, *The Philadelphia Negro: A Social Study* (Philadelphia: University of Pennsylvania, 1995; orig. pub. 1889); Earl Wright, "Using the Master's Tools: The Atlanta Sociological Laboratory and American Sociology, 1896–1924," *Sociological Spectrum* 22, no. 1 (2002): 15–39.

17. Clifton Conrad and Marybeth Gasman, *Educating a Diverse Nation: Lessons from Minority Serving Institutions* (Cambridge, MA: Harvard University Press, 2015); Gasman, *Envisioning Black Colleges*.

18. Thelin, *History of American Higher Education;* James D. Anderson, "Race, Meritocracy, and the American Academy during the Immediate Post–World War II Era," *History of Education Quarterly* 33, no. 2 (1993): 151–175.

19. Jason L. Riley, "Black Colleges Need a New Mission," *Wall Street Journal,* September 28, 2010; Marybeth Gasman, "Salvaging 'Academic Disaster Areas': The Black College Response to Christopher Jencks and David Riesman's 1967 *Harvard Educational Review* Article," *Journal of Higher Education* 77, no. 2 (2006): 317–352.

20. Ibid.

21. Marybeth Gasman and Louis W. Sullivan, *The Morehouse Mystique: Becoming a Doctor at the Nation's Newest African American Medical School* (Baltimore: Johns Hopkins University Press, 2012); Marybeth Gasman and Thai-Huy Nguyen, "Historically Black Colleges and Universities (HBCUs): Leading Our Nation's Effort to Improve the Science, Technology, Engineering, and Mathematics (STEM) Pipeline," *Texas Education Review* 2, no. 1 (2014).

22. Melvin C. Terrell, "Racism: Undermining Higher Education," *NASPA Journal* 26, no. 2 (1988): 82–84; Daniel G. Solorzano and Octavio Villalpando, "Critical Race Theory, Marginality, and the Experience of Students of Color in Higher Education," *Sociology of Education: Emerging Perspectives* (1998): 211–224.

23. "HBCUs: Segregated, but Not Segregating," *Diverse,* March 4, 2009, http://diverseeducation.com/article/12348.

24. Jacques Steinberg, *The Gatekeepers: Inside the Admissions Process of a Premier College* (New York: Penguin Books, 2003); Daniel Golden, *The Price of Admission: How America's Ruling Class Buys Its Way into Elite Colleges—and Who Gets Left Outside the Gates* (New York: Broadway Books, 2007); Jerome Karabel, *The Chosen: The Hidden History of Admission and Exclusion at Harvard, Yale, and Princeton* (New York: Mariner, 2006).

25. Doug Lederman and Scott Jaschik, "Federal Accountability and Financial Pressure: A Survey of Presidents," *Inside Higher Education*, March 7, 2014; Marybeth Gasman, "Presidents in Denial," *Inside Higher Education*, March 31, 2014.

26. "Campus Demands," The Demands, accessed June 23, 2017, http://www.thedemands.org.

27. Alexander, *The New Jim Crow*.

28. John P. Jackson and Nadine M. Weidman, *Race, Racism, and Science: Social Impact and Interaction* (New Brunswick, NJ: Rutgers University Press, 2005).

29. Frances Maher and Mary Kay Thompson Tetreault, "Learning in the Dark: How Assumptions of Whiteness Shape Classroom Knowledge," *Harvard Educational Review* 67, no. 2 (1997): 321–350; Annie Howell and Frank Tuitt, *Race and Higher Education: Rethinking Pedagogy in Diverse College Classrooms*, Harvard Educational Review Reprint Series (Cambridge, MA: Harvard Education Publishing, 2003); Nelson M. Rodriguez and Leila E. Villaverde, *Dismantling White Privilege: Pedagogy, Politics, and Whiteness*, vol. 73 of *Counterpoints: Studies in the Postmodern Theory of Education* (New York: Peter Lang, 2000): 275; Guillermo Rebollo-Gil and Amanda Moras, "Defining an 'Anti'stance: Key Pedagogical Questions about Engaging Anti-racism in College Classrooms," *Race Ethnicity and Education* 9, no. 4 (2006): 381–394.

30. Terrell L. Strayhorn, *College Students' Sense of Belonging: A Key to Educational Success for All Students* (New York: Routledge, 2012); Joe R. Feagin,

Hernan Vera, and Nikitah Imani, *The Agony of Education: Black Students at White Colleges and Universities* (New York: Psychology Press, 1996); Walter R. Allen, Edgar G. Epps, and Nesha Z. Haniff, *College in Black and White: African American Students in Predominantly White and in Historically Black Public Universities* (Albany: SUNY Press, 1991).

31. Marybeth Gasman, "An Ivy League Professor on Why Colleges Don't Hire More Faculty of Color: 'We Don't Want Them,'" *Washington Post*, September 26, 2016; Caroline Sotello Viernes Turner and Samuel L. Myers, *Faculty of Color in Academe: Bittersweet Success* (New York: Allyn and Bacon, 2000).

32. D. Cohn and A. Caumont, "Demographic Trends That Are Shaping the U.S. and the World," *FactTank,* March 31, 2016, 10.

33. Turner and Myers, *Faculty of Color in Academe;* Aaron Clauset, Samuel Arbesman, and Daneile Larremore, "Systematic Inequality and Hierarchy in Faculty Hiring Networks," *Science Advances* 1, no. 1 (2015).

34. Julie R. Posselt, *Inside Graduate Admissions: Merit, Diversity, and Faculty Gatekeeping* (Cambridge, MA: Harvard University Press, 2016).

35. Bonilla-Silva, *Racism without Racists.*

36. Anthony P. Carnevale and Jeff Strohl, "Separate and Unequal: How Higher Education Reinforces the Intergenerational Reproduction of White Racial Privilege," Georgetown University Center on Education and the Workforce, 2013, https://cew.georgetown.edu/cew-reports/separate-unequal/.

37. Bonilla-Silva, *Racism without Racists;* Eduardo Bonilla-Silva, *White Supremacy and Racism in the Post–Civil Rights Era* (New York: Lynne Rienner, 2001); William A. Smith, Tara J. Yosso, and Daniel G. Solórzano, "Racial Primes and Black Misandry on Historically White Campuses: Toward Critical Race Accountability in Educational Administration," *Educational Administration Quarterly* 43, no. 5 (2007): 559–585; Donald B. Pope-Davis and Thomas M. Ottavi, "The Relationship between Racism

and Racial Identity among White Americans: A Replication and Extension," *Journal of Counseling and Development* 72, no. 3 (1994): 293–297.

38. Aldon D. Morris, "The State of Sociology: The Case for Systemic Change," *Social Problems* 64, no. 2 (2017): 206–211.

39. Valerie Strauss, "Enrollments Surge at Historically Black Colleges amid Rise in Racial Tensions," *Washington Post,* September 11, 2016.

40. Marie-Elena Reyes, "Unique Challenges for Women of Color in STEM Transferring from Community Colleges to Universities," *Harvard Educational Review* 81, no. 2 (2001); Alberto F. Cabrera, Amaury Nora, Patrick T. Terenzini, Ernest Pascarella, and Linda Serra Hagedorn, "Campus Racial Climate and the Adjustment of Students to College: A Comparison between White Students and African-American Students," *Journal of Higher Education* 70, no. 2 (1999); Kenneth Maton and Freeman Hrabowski, "Increasing the Number of African American PhDs in the Sciences and Engineering: A Strengths-Based Approach," *American Psychologist* 59, no. 6 (2004).

41. Jacqueline Fleming, *Blacks in College: A Comparative Study of Students' Success in Black and in White Institutions* (San Francisco: Jossey-Bass, 1985); Walter Allen, "The Color of Success: African-American College Student Outcomes at Predominantly White and Historically Black Public Colleges and Universities," *Harvard Educational Review* 62, no. 1 (1992): 26–45; Allen, Epps, and Haniff, *College in Black and White;* Lemuel Watson and George D. Kuh, "The Influence of Dominant Race Environments on Student Involvement, Perceptions, and Educational Gains: A Look at Historically Black and Predominantly White Liberal Arts Institutions," *Journal of College Student Development* 37, no. 4 (1996): 415–424; Melody L. Russell and Mary M. Atwater, "Traveling the Road to Success: A Discourse on Persistence throughout the Science Pipeline with African American Students at a Predominantly White Institution," *Journal of Research in Science Teaching* 42, no. 6 (2005): 691–715.

42. See Appendix for more details on the individual HBCUs and an explanation of our research approach. Please note that all names are pseudonyms in this book with the exception of the presidents of the ten HBCUs.

43. Carl Wieman, *Improving How Universities Teach Science: Lessons from the Science Education Initiative* (Cambridge, MA: Harvard University Press, 2017).

44. Gasman, *Envisioning Black Colleges.*

1. THE STATE OF STEM IN THE UNITED STATES

1. National Research Council, *Successful K–12 STEM Education: Identifying Effective Approaches in Science, Technology, Engineering, and Mathematics* (Washington, DC: National Academies Press, 2011); Karen Humes, Nicholas A. Jones, and Roberto R. Ramirez, *Overview of Race and Hispanic Origin, 2010* (Washington, DC: U.S. Department of Commerce, Economics and Statistics Administration, U.S. Census Bureau, 2011).

2. National Science Foundation, National Center for Science and Engineering Statistics, special tabulations of U.S. Department of Education, National Center for Education, "Statistics, Integrated Postsecondary Education Data System, Completions Survey," 2016, table 5-6. We use "African Americans" and "Blacks" in discussing the descriptive data as it echoes the categories used by the National Science Foundation, the agency that compiles this data.

3. Marybeth Gasman, "The Changing Face of Historically Black Colleges and Universities," Penn Center for Minority Serving Institutions, 2013, https://repository.upenn.edu/gse_pubs/335.

4. National Science Foundation, "Completions Survey," table 5-8.

5. Douglas S. Massey, *Categorically Unequal: The American Stratification System* (New York: Russell Sage Foundation, 2007).

6. Statista, "Percentage of Students Who Received Pell Grants in the United States in 2015, by Race," https://www.statista.com/statistics/708249/stu dents-receiving-pell-grants-by-race-us/.

7. U.S. Department of Education, Institute of Education Sciences, National Center for Education Statistics, "Number and Percentage of Children under Age 18 Living in Poverty, by Family Structure and Race / Ethnicity with Selected Subgroups: 2007 and 2012," 2014, http:// nces.ed.gov/programs/digest/d13/tables/dt13_102.60.asp.

8. William Julius Wilson, *The Truly Disadvantaged: The Inner City, the Underclass, and Public Policy* (Chicago: University of Chicago Press, 2012); Valerie Strauss, "Enrollments Surge at Historically Black Colleges amid Rise in Racial Tensions," *Washington Post*, September 11, 2016.

9. Drew Desilver, "Black Unemployment Rate Is Consistently Twice That of Whites," Pew Research Center, August 21, 2013.

10. Douglas S. Massey, Andrew B. Gross, and Kumiko Shibuya, "Migration, Segregation, and the Geographic Concentration of Poverty," *American Sociological Review* (1994): 425–445; Mario Luis Small and Katherine Newman, "Urban Poverty after the Truly Disadvantaged: The Rediscovery of the Family, the Neighborhood, and Culture," *Annual Review of Sociology* 27, no. 1 (2001): 23–45.

11. Camille Zubrinsky Charles, "The Dynamics of Racial Residential Segregation," *Annual Review of Sociology* 29, no. 1 (2003): 167–207.

12. Sean F. Reardon, John T. Yun, and Michal Kurlaender, "Implications of Income-Based School Assignment Policies for Racial School Segregation," *Educational Evaluation and Policy Analysis* 28, no. 1 (2006): 49–75; John T. Yun and Sean Reardon, "Private School Racial Enrollments and Segregation," in *School Choice and Diversity: What the Evidence Says*, ed. Janelle T. Scott (New York: Teachers College Press, 2005).

13. Annette Lareau, *Unequal Childhoods: Class, Race, and Family Life* (San Francisco: University of California Press, 2011); Douglas S. Massey,

Camille Z. Charles, Garvey Lundy, and Mary J. Fischer, *The Source of the River: The Social Origins of Freshmen at America's Selective Colleges and Universities* (Princeton, NJ: Princeton University Press, 2011).

14. Massey et al., *Source of the River*.

15. Catherine Compton-Lilly, *Reading Families: The Literate Lives of Urban Children* (New York: Teachers College Press, 2003); Shirley Brice Heath, *Ways with Words: Language, Life and Work in Communities and Classrooms* (New York: Cambridge University Press, 1983).

16. Elizabeth A. Armstrong and Laura T. Hamilton, *Paying for the Party* (Cambridge, MA: Harvard University Press, 2013); Pierre Bourdieu and Jean-Claude Passeron, *Reproduction in Education, Society and Culture* (San Francisco: Sage, 1990); Lareau, *Unequal Childhoods*.

17. Lareau, *Unequal Childhoods*.

18. Trevor Tompson, Jennifer Benz, and Jennifer Agiesta, "Parents' Attitudes on the Quality of Education in the United States," Associated Press-NORC Center for Public Affairs Research, 2013, http://www.apnorc.org/PDFs/Parent%20Attitudes/AP_NORC_Parents%20Attitudes%20on%20the%20Quality%20of%20Education%20in%20the%20US_FINAL_2.pdf.

19. John B. Diamond, "Beyond Social Class: Cultural Resources and Educational Participation among Low-Income Black Parents," *Berkeley Journal of Sociology* (1999): 15–54.

20. Sarah Crafter and Rachel Maunder, "Understanding Transitions Using a Sociocultural Framework," *Educational and Child Psychology* 29, no. 1 (2012): 10–18; Massey et al., *Source of the River*; William H. Sewell, Archibald O. Haller, and Alejandro Portes, "The Educational and Early Occupational Attainment Process," *American Sociological Review* (1969): 82–92.

21. Patricia M. McDonough, *Choosing Colleges: How Social Class and Schools Structure Opportunity* (Albany: SUNY Press, 1997); Lareau, *Unequal Childhoods*.

22. National Center for Education Statistics, "Number of Undergraduate Students Enrolled in the United States from 1976 to 2016, by Ethnicity (in 1,000)," https://www.statista.com/statistics/236489/undergraduate-enrollment-by-ethnicity-in-the-us/; Grace Kao and Jennifer S. Thompson, "Racial and Ethnic Stratification in Educational Achievement and Attainment," *Annual Review of Sociology* 29, no. 1 (2003): 417–442.

23. Robert Teranishi, Walter Allen, Daniel G. Solorzano, and Renee Smith Maddox, "Separate but Certainly Not Equal: 2003 CAPAA Findings," Ralph J. Bunche Center for African American Studies, University of California Los Angeles (2004).

24. Leslie S. Kaplan and William A. Owings, "Teacher Quality and Student Achievement: Recommendations for Principals" *NASSP Bulletin* 85, no. 628 (2001): 64–73; Daniel G. Solorzano and Armida Ornelas, "A Critical Race Analysis of Latina / o and African American Advanced Placement Enrollment in Public High Schools," *High School Journal* 87, no. 3 (2004): 15–26.

25. John T. Yun and José F. Moreno, "College Access, K–12 Concentrated Disadvantage, and the Next 25 Years of Education Research," *Educational Researcher* 35, no. 1 (2006): 12–19.

26. Michael Neuschatz and Mark McFarling, *Maintaining Momentum: High School Physics for a New Millennium—AIP Report* (College Park, MD: American Institute of Physics, Education and Employment Statistics Division, 1999).

27. McDonough, *Choosing Colleges*.

28. Yun and Moreno, "College Access," 13.

29. Jon Hurwitz and Mark Peffley, "Public Perceptions of Race and Crime: The Role of Racial Stereotypes," *American Journal of Political Science* (1997): 375–401.

30. Elijah Anderson, *Against the Wall: Poor, Young, Black, and Male* (Philadelphia: University of Pennsylvania Press, 2008); Katherine S. Newman, *No Shame in My Game: The Working Poor in the Inner City* (New York: Vintage,

2009); Carol B. Stack, *All Our Kin: Strategies for Survival in a Black Community* (New York: Basic Books, 1975).

31. Robin Nicole Johnson-Ahorlu, "'Our Biggest Challenge Is Stereotypes': Understanding Stereotype Threat and the Academic Experiences of African American Undergraduates," *Journal of Negro Education* 82, no. 4 (2013): 382–392; Edward Taylor and James Soto Antony, "Stereotype Threat Reduction and Wise Schooling: Towards the Successful Socialization of African American Doctoral Students in Education," *Journal of Negro Education* (2000): 184–198; Yu Xie and Alexandra A. Killewald, *Is American Science in Decline?* (Cambridge, MA: Harvard University Press, 2012).

32. Oren L. McClain, "Negotiating Identity: A Look at the Educational Experiences of Black Undergraduates in STEM Disciplines," *Peabody Journal of Education* 89, no. 3 (2014): 380–392.

33. Elaine Seymour and Nancy M. Hewitt, *Talking about Leaving: Why Undergraduates Leave the Sciences* (Boulder, CO: Westview, 1997).

34. Ibid.

35. Lois Powell, "Factors Associated with the Underrepresentation of African Americans in Mathematics and Science," *Journal of Negro Education* 59, no. 3 (1990): 292–298, at 296.

36. Ryan P. Brown and Monica N. Lee, "Stigma Consciousness and the Race Gap in College Academic Achievement," *Self and Identity* 4, no. 2 (2005): 149–157.

37. Melody L. Russell and Mary M. Atwater, "Traveling the Road to Success: A Discourse on Persistence throughout the Science Pipeline with African American Students at a Predominantly White Institution," *Journal of Research in Science Teaching* 42, no. 6 (2005): 691–715.

38. Ericka J. Fisher, "Black Student Achievement and the Oppositional Culture Model," *Journal of Negro Education* (2005): 201–209.

39. Claude M. Steele and Joshua Aronson, "Stereotype Threat and the Intellectual Test Performance of African Americans," *Journal of Personality and Social Psychology* 69, no. 5 (1995): 797.

40. National Academy of Sciences, National Academy of Engineering, and Institute of Medicine, *Expanding Underrepresented Minority Participation: America's Science and Technology Talent at the Crossroads* (Washington, DC: National Academies Press, 2011).

41. Catherine Good, Joshua Aronson, and Michael Inzlicht, "Improving Adolescents' Standardized Test Performance: An Intervention to Reduce the Effects of Stereotype Threat," *Journal of Applied Developmental Psychology* 24, no. 6 (2003): 645–662.

42. Ibid.

43. Alexander W. Astin and Helen S. Astin, "Undergraduate Science Education: The Impact of Different College Environments on the Educational Pipeline in the Sciences—Final Report" (1992), https://eric.ed.gov/?id=ED362404; Donald A. Barr, *Questioning the Premedical Paradigm: Enhancing Diversity in the Medical Profession a Century after the Flexner Report* (Baltimore: Johns Hopkins University Press, 2010); Jeannie Oakes et al., "Multiplying Inequalities: The Effects of Race, Social Class, and Tracking on Opportunities to Learn Mathematics and Science" (1990), https://eric.ed.gov/?id=ED329615; Kao and Thompson, "Racial and Ethnic Stratification."

44. Oakes et al., "Multiplying Inequalities."

45. Philip M. Sadler and Robert H. Tai, "Success in Introductory College Physics: The Role of High School Preparation," *Science Education* 85, no. 2 (2001): 111–136.

46. Will Tyson, "Modeling Engineering Degree Attainment Using High School and College Physics and Calculus Course Taking and Achievement," *Journal of Engineering Education* 100, no. 4 (2011): 760–777.

47. Massey et al., *Source of the River;* Catherine Riegle-Crumb and Eric Grodsky, "Racial-Ethnic Differences at the Intersection of Math Course-Taking and Achievement," *Sociology of Education* 83, no. 3 (2010): 248–270.

48. U.S. Department of Education, National Center for Education Statistics, "High School Transcript Study (HSTS)" (1990, 2000, 2005, and 2009), https://nces.ed.gov/programs/digest/d16/tables/dt16_225.40.asp.

49. Barr, *Questioning the Premedical Paradigm.*

50. Adam V. Maltese and Robert H. Tai, "Pipeline Persistence: Examining the Association of Educational Experiences with Earned Degrees in STEM among U.S. Students," *Science Education* 95, no. 5 (2011): 877–907; Will Tyson, Reginald Lee, Kathryn M. Borman, and Mary Ann Hanson, "Science, Technology, Engineering, and Mathematics (STEM) Pathways: High School Science and Math Coursework and Postsecondary Degree Attainment," *Journal of Education for Students Placed at Risk* 12, no. 3 (2007): 243–270; Seymour and Hewitt, *Talking about Leaving.*

51. Catherine Riegle-Crumb and Barbara King, "Questioning a White Male Advantage in STEM: Examining Disparities in College Major by Gender and Race / Ethnicity," *Educational Researcher* 39, no. 9 (2010): 656–664.

52. Thomas L. Hilton and Valerie E. Lee, "Student Interest and Persistence in Science: Changes in the Educational Pipeline in the Last Decade," *Journal of Higher Education* 59, no. 5 (1988): 510–526; National Science Foundation, "Women, Minorities, and Persons with Disabilities in Science and Engineering," 2011, tables 2-8 and 5-6, https://www.nsf.gov/statistics/2017/nsf17310/; Seymour and Hewitt, *Talking about Leaving;* Riegle-Crumb and King, "Questioning a White Male Advantage."

53. Barr, *Questioning the Premedical Paradigm;* Sylvia Hurtado, Christopher B. Newman, Minh C. Tran, and Mitchell J. Chang, "Improving the Rate of Success for Underrepresented Racial Minorities in STEM Fields: Insights from a National Project," *New Directions for Institutional Research* 148 (2010): 5–15.

54. American Association for the Advancement of Science, *Benchmarks for Science Literacy* (New York: Oxford University Press, 1993).

55. Jay B. Labov, "From the National Academies: The Challenges and Opportunities for Improving Undergraduate Science Education through Introductory Courses," *Cell Biology Education* 3, no. 4 (2004): 212–214, at 213.

56. Charles Alexander, Eric Chen, and Kevin Grumbach, "How Leaky Is the Health Career Pipeline? Minority Student Achievement in College Gateway Courses," *Academic Medicine* 84, no. 6 (2009): 797–802.

57. Donald A. Barr, Maria Elena Gonzalez, and Stanley F. Wanat, "The Leaky Pipeline: Factors Associated with Early Decline in Interest in Premedical Studies among Underrepresented Minority Undergraduate Students," *Academic Medicine* 83, no. 5 (2008): 503–511.

58. Alexander, Chen, and Grumbach, "How Leaky Is the Health Career Pipeline?," 801.

59. Seymour and Hewitt, *Talking about Leaving*.

60. Hurtado, Newman, Tran, and Chang, "Improving the Rate of Success," 10.

61. Barr, *Questioning the Premedical Paradigm*.

62. M. Kevin Eagan, Gina A. Garcia, Sylvia Hurtado, and Josephine A. Gasiewski, "Passing through the Gates: Identifying and Developing Talent in Introductory STEM Courses," UCLA, 2012, https://heri.ucla.edu/nih/downloads/AERA2012EaganPassingthroughtheGates.pdf.

2. INSTITUTIONAL RESPONSIBILITY

1. John R. Thelin, *A History of American Higher Education* (Baltimore: Johns Hopkins University Press, 2011).

2. Jerome Karabel, *The Chosen: The Hidden History of Admission and Exclusion at Harvard, Yale, and Princeton* (New York: Houghton Mifflin Harcourt, 2006).

3. Ibid.

4. Clifton Conrad and Marybeth Gasman, *Educating a Diverse Nation: Lessons from Minority Serving Institutions* (Cambridge, MA: Harvard University Press, 2015).

5. Derald Wing Sue, Christina M. Capodilupo, and Aisha Holder, "Racial Microaggressions in the Life Experience of Black Americans," *Professional Psychology: Research and Practice* 39, no. 3 (2008): 329; Susan Rakosi Rosenbloom and Niobe Way, "Experiences of Discrimination among African American, Asian American, and Latino Adolescents in an Urban High School," *Youth & Society* 35, no. 4 (2004): 420–451.

6. Sharon L. Fries-Britt and Bridget Turner, "Facing Stereotypes: A Case Study of Black Students on a White Campus," *Journal of College Student Development* 42, no. 5 (2001), 420.

7. Ronald F. Ferguson, "Teachers' Perceptions and Expectations and the Black-White Test Score Gap," *Urban Education* 38, no. 4 (2003): 460–507.

8. Daniel Solorzano, "Images and Words That Wound: Critical Race Theory, Racial Stereotyping, and Teacher Education," *Teacher Education Quarterly* (1997): 5–19.

9. David T. Conley, "Redefining College Readiness," Educational Policy Improvement Center, 2007, https://eric.ed.gov/?id=ED539251.

10. Ibid.

11. U.S. Department of Education, National Center for Education Statistics, High School and Beyond Longitudinal Study of 1980 Sophomores (HS&B-So:80 / 82), "High School Transcript Study"; and 1990, 1994, 1998, 2000, 2005, and 2009 High School Transcript Study (HSTS), 2011, https://nces.ed.gov/programs/digest/d11/tables/xls/tabn161.xls.

12. Marybeth Gasman and Thai-Huy Nguyen, "Historically Black Colleges and Universities (HBCUs): Leading Our Nation's Effort to Improve the Science, Technology, Engineering, and Mathematics (STEM) Pipeline," Penn Center for Minority Serving Institutions, 2014.

13. Camille Zubrinsky Charles, "The Dynamics of Racial Residential Segregation," *Annual Review of Sociology* 29, no. 1 (2003): 167–207.

14. Karl Alexander, Doris Entwisle, and Linda Olson, *The Long Shadow: Family Background, Disadvantaged Urban Youth, and the Transition to Adulthood* (New York: Russell Sage Foundation, 2014).

15. Joshua Aronson, Carrie B. Fried, and Catherine Good, "Reducing the Effects of Stereotype Threat on African American College Students by Shaping Theories of Intelligence," *Journal of Experimental Social Psychology* 38, no. 2 (2002): 113–125; Claude M. Steele, *Whistling Vivaldi: How Stereotypes Affect Us and What We Can Do (Issues of Our Time)* (New York: W. W. Norton, 2011).

16. Richard E. Mayer, "Rote versus Meaningful Learning," *Theory into Practice* 41, no. 4 (2002): 226–232.

17. Susan Bobbitt Nolen and Thomas M. Haladyna, "Motivation and Studying in High School Science," *Journal of Research in Science Teaching* 27, no. 2 (1990): 115–126.

18. Solorzano, "Images and Words That Wound."

19. Steele, *Whistling Vivaldi.*

20. Fries-Britt and Turner, "Facing Stereotypes."

21. Carol S. Dweck, *Mindset: The New Psychology of Success* (New York: Ballantine Books, 2007).

22. Charles, "Dynamics of Racial Residential Segregation"; Grace Kao and Jennifer S. Thompson, "Racial and Ethnic Stratification in Educational Achievement and Attainment," *Annual Review of Sociology* (2003): 417–442.

23. Ibid.

24. Mary E. Pritchard and Gregory S. Wilson, "Using Emotional and Social Factors to Predict Student Success," *Journal of College Student Development* 44, no. 1 (2003).

25. John Diamond, "Race and White Supremacy in the Sociology of Education: Shifting the Intellectual Gaze," in *Education in a New Society: Re-
viewing the Sociology of Education*, ed. S. Davies and J. Mehta (Chicago:
University of Chicago Press, 2018), 345.

26. Ebony O. McGee and Danny B. Martin, "'You Would Not Believe What
I Have to Go Through to Prove My Intellectual Value!': Stereotype
Management among Academically Successful Black Mathematics and
Engineering Students," *American Educational Research Journal* 48, no. 6
(2011): 1347–1389.

3. PEER-TO-PEER SUPPORT AND INTELLECTUAL GENEROSITY

1. National Science Foundation, *Women, Minorities, and Persons with Disabilities in the Sciences and Engineering* (Arlington, VA: National Science
Foundation, 2014), table 2-8.

2. Ibid.

3. Elaine Seymour and Nancy M. Hewitt, *Talking about Leaving: Why Undergraduates Leave the Sciences* (Boulder, CO: Westview, 1997).

4. Ibid.

5. Roger G. Baldwin, "The Climate for Undergraduate Teaching and
Learning in STEM Fields," *New Directions for Teaching and Learning* 2009,
no. 117 (2009): 9–17.

6. Robert T. Palmer, Dina C. Maramba, and Marybeth Gasman, eds., *Fostering Success of Ethnic and Racial Minorities in STEM* (New York: Routledge Press, 2013).

7. Uri Treisman, "Studying Students Studying Calculus: A Look at the
lives of Minority Mathematics Students in College," *College Mathematics
Journal* 23, no. 5 (1992): 362–372; Robert E. Fullilove and Uri Treisman,
"Mathematics Achievement among African American Undergraduates

at the University of California, Berkeley: An Evaluation of the Mathe-matics Workshop Program," *Journal of Negro Education* 59, no. 3 (1990): 463–478.

8. Thomas L. Hilton and Valerie E. Lee, "Student Interest and Persistence in Science: Changes in the Educational Pipeline in the Last Decade," *Journal of Higher Education* 59, no. 5 (1988): 510–526.

9. Ibid.

10. Nicole M. Stephens, Stephanie A. Fryberg, Hazel Rose Markus, Ca-mille S. Johnson, and Rebecca Covarrubias, "Unseen Disadvantage: How American Universities' Focus on Independence Undermines the Aca-demic Performance of First-Generation College Students," *Journal of Personality and Social Psychology* 102, no. 6 (2012): 1178.

4. MESSAGES AND EXAMPLES OF INHERENT INCLUSIVITY

1. Marybeth Gasman, *Envisioning Black Colleges: A History of the United Negro College Fund* (Baltimore: Johns Hopkins University Press, 2007); Clifton Conrad and Marybeth Gasman, *Educating a Diverse Nation: Les-sons from Minority Serving Institutions* (Cambridge, MA: Harvard Univer-sity Press, 2015).

2. Terrell L. Strayhorn, *College Students' Sense of Belonging: A Key to Educa-tional Success for All Students* (New York: Routledge, 2012).

3. Elaine Seymour and Nancy M. Hewitt, *Talking about Leaving: Why Un-dergraduates Leave the Sciences* (Boulder, CO: Westview, 1997); Roger G. Baldwin, "The Climate for Undergraduate Teaching and Learning in STEM Fields," *New Directions for Teaching and Learning*, no. 117 (2009): 9–17.

4. Gasman, *Envisioning Black Colleges*; Henry Drewry and Humphrey Do-ermann, *Stand and Prosper: Private Black Colleges and Their Students* (Princeton, NJ: Princeton University Press, 2001).

5. Ebony O. McGee and Danny B. Martin, "'You Would Not Believe What I Have to Go Through to Prove My Intellectual Value!': Stereotype Management among Academically Successful Black Mathematics and Engineering Students," *American Educational Research Journal* 48, no. 6 (2011): 1347–1389.

6. Marybeth Gasman and Louis W. Sullivan, *The Morehouse Mystique: Becoming a Doctor at the Nation's Newest Black Medical School* (Baltimore: Johns Hopkins University Press, 2012); Darlene C. Hine, *Black Women in White: Racial Conflict and Cooperation in the Nursing Profession, 1890–1950* (Bloomington: Indiana University Press, 1989).

7. Ronald Takaki, *A Different Mirror: A History of Multicultural America*, rev. ed. (New York: Back Bay Books, 2012).

8. Gasman and Sullivan, *Morehouse Mystique*.

9. "Section II: Current Status of the U.S. Physician Workforce," AAMC Facts & Figures 2016, Interactive Report, Section II, "Current Status of the US Physician Workforce," Comments, http://aamcdiversityfactsandfigures .org.

10. "Applicants, by Undergraduate Institutions: Tables," AAMC Facts & Figures 2016, table 14, http://www.aamcdiversityfactsandfigures2016.org /report-section/undergraduate-institutions/; National Center for Education Statistics, College Navigator, "Xavier University of Louisiana," https://nces.ed.gov/collegenavigator/?q=xavier%2Buniversity&s =all&id=160904.

11. Nikole Hannah Jones, "A Prescription for More Black Doctors, *New York Times*, September 9, 2015.

12. "Current Trends in Medical Education," AAMC Facts & Figures 2016, http://www.aamcdiversityfactsandfigures2016.org.

13. "Applicants, by Undergraduate Institutions: Tables."

14. Daniel Solorzano, Miguel Ceja, and Tara Yosso, "Critical Race Theory, Racial Microaggressions, and Campus Racial Climate: The Experiences

of African American College Students," *Journal of Negro Education* (2000): 60–73.

15. Conrad and Gasman, *Educating a Diverse Nation*.

16. Margaret Cahalan and Laura Perna, *Indicators of Higher Education Equity in the United States: 45 Year Trend Report* (New York: Pell Institute, 2015); Julie R. Posselt, *Inside Graduate Admissions: Merit, Diversity, and Faculty Gatekeeping* (Cambridge, MA: Harvard University Press, 2016).

17. Conrad and Gasman, *Educating a Diverse Nation*.

18. Ibid.

5. STUDENTS' NEEDS OVER FACULTY MEMBERS' NEEDS

1. Sheila Slaughter and Gary Rhoades, *Academic Capitalism and the New Economy: Markets, State, and Higher Education* (Baltimore: Johns Hopkins University Press, 2004).

2. Julie R. Posselt, *Inside Graduate Admissions: Merit, Diversity, and Faculty Gatekeeping* (Cambridge, MA: Harvard University Press, 2016); Ann E. Austin, "Preparing the Next Generation of Faculty: Graduate School as Socialization to the Academic Career," *Journal of Higher Education* 73, no. 1 (2002): 94–122; Susan K. Gardner, "Fitting the Mold of Graduate School: A Qualitative Study of Socialization in Doctoral Education," *Innovative Higher Education* 33, no. 2 (2008): 125–138.

3. Jana Bouwma-Gearhart, "Research University STEM Faculty Members' Motivation to Engage in Teaching Professional Development: Building the Choir through an Appeal to Extrinsic Motivation and Ego," *Journal of Science Education and Technology* 21, no. 5 (2012): 558–570; Melanie M. Cooper et al., "Challenge Faculty to Transform STEM Learning," *Science* 350 (2015): 281–282.

4. Laura Perna, Valerie Lundy-Wagner, Noah D. Drezner, Marybeth Gasman, Susan Yoon, Enakshi Bose, and Shannon Garry, "The Contribu-

tions of HBCUs to the Preparation of African American Women for STEM Careers: A Case Study," *Research in Higher Education* 50, no. 1 (2009); Marybeth Gasman, Thai-Huy Nguyen, Clifton Conrad, Todd Lundberg, and Felecia Commodore, "Black Male Success in STEM: A Case Study of Morehouse College," *Journal of Diversity in Higher Education* 10, no. 2 (2017).

5. Slaughter and Rhoades, *Academic Capitalism.*

6. George Dawson, "Xavier University Premedicine Program's Prescription for Success: An Interview with JW Carmichael Jr., MS, PHD," *Journal of the National Medical Association* 97, no. 9 (2005): 1294–1300, at 1299.

7. Deborah Olsen and Janet P. Near, "Role Conflict and Faculty Life Satisfaction," *Review of Higher Education* 17, no. 2 (1994).

8. Perna et al., "The Contributions of HBCUs"; Gasman et al., "Black Male Success in STEM."

6. SAME-GENDER, SAME-RACE FACULTY ROLE MODELS

1. National Center for Education Statistics, "Instructional Staff with Faculty Status," 2016, https://nces.ed.gov/fastfacts/display.asp?id=61.

2. National Science Foundation, *Women, Minorities, and Persons with Disabilities in the Sciences and Engineering* (Arlington, VA: National Science Foundation, 2015), table 9-25.

3. Ibid.

4. Lenoar Foster, "The Not-So-Invisible Professors: White Faculty at the Black College," *Urban Education* 36, no. 5 (2001): 611–629; Lenoar Foster, Janet A. Guyden, and Andrea L. Miller, *Affirmed Action: Essays on the Academic and Social Lives of White Faculty Members at Historically Black Colleges and Universities* (New York; Rowman and Littlefield, 1999).

5. Maya A. Beasley and Mary J. Fischer, "Why They Leave: The Impact of Stereotype Threat on the Attrition of Women and Minorities from Sci-

ence, Math and Engineering Majors," *Social Psychology of Education* (2012): 1–22.

6. Daniel Solorzano, Miguel Ceja, and Tara Yosso, "Critical Race Theory, Racial Microaggressions, and Campus Racial Climate: The Experiences of African American College Students," *Journal of Negro Education* (2000): 60–73.

7. Jioni A. Lewis, Ruby Mendenhall, Stacy A. Harwood, and Margaret Browne Huntt, "'Ain't I a Woman?': Perceived Gendered Racial Microaggressions Experienced by Black Women," *Counseling Psychologist* 44, no. 5 (2016): 758–780.

8. Benjamin Drury, John Oliver Siy, and Sapna Cheryan, "When Do Female Role Models Benefit Women? The Importance of Differentiating Recruitment from Retention in STEM," *Psychological Inquiry* 22, no. 4 (2011): 265–269; Shannon E. Holleran, Jessica Whitehead, Toni Schmader, and Matthias R. Mehl, "Talking Shop and Shooting the Breeze: A Study of Workplace Conversation and Job Disengagement among STEM Faculty," *Social Psychological and Personality Science* 2, no. 1 (2011): 65–71.

9. Gloria Ladson-Billings, "'Who You Callin' Nappy-Headed?': A Critical Race Theory Look at the Construction of Black Women," *Race Ethnicity and Education* 12, no. 1 (2009): 87–99.

10. William H. Robinson, Ebony O. McGee, Lydia C. Bentley, Stacey L. Houston II, and Portia K. Botchway, "Addressing Negative Racial and Gendered Experiences That Discourage Academic Careers in Engineering," *Best of Respect*, March / April 2016.

11. Harold E. Cheatham and Christine E. Phelps, "Promoting the Development of Graduate Students of Color," *New Directions for Student Services* 72 (1995): 91–99; Alberto F. Cabrera, Carol L. Colbeck, and Patrick T. Terenzini, "Developing Performance Indicators for Assessing Classroom Teaching Practices and Student Learning," *Research in Higher Education* 42, no. 3 (2001): 327–352; Sylvia Hurtado, M. Kevin Eagan, Nolan Cabrera,

Monica Lin, Julie Park, and Miguel Lopez, "Training Future Scientists: Predicting First-Year Minority Student Participation in Health Science Research," *Research in Higher Education* 49, no. 2 (2008): 126–152.

12. Kevin N. Rask and Elizabeth M. Bailey, "Are Faculty Role Models? Evidence from Major Choice in an Undergraduate Institution," *Journal of Economic Education* 33, no. 2 (2002): 99–124.

13. Anna J. Egalite, Brian Kisida, and Marcus A. Winters, "Representation in the Classroom: The Effect of Own-Race Teachers on Student Achievement," *Economics of Education Review* 45 (2015): 44–52.

14. Fang-Yi Flora Wei and Katherine Grace Hendrix, "Minority and Majority Faculty Members in a Historically Black College / University: Redefining Professors' Teacher Credibility and Classroom Management," *Qualitative Research Reports in Communication* 17, no. 1 (2016): 102–111.

15. Ibid.

16. Marybeth Gasman et al., *Minority Serving Institutions*, ASHE Monograph Series (San Francisco: Jossey-Bass, 2018).

17. Lezli Baskerville, L. Berger, and Lionel Smith, "The Role of Historically Black Colleges and Universities in Faculty Diversity," *American Academic* 4, no. 1 (2008): 11–31.

18. Foster, "The Not-So-Invisible Professors"; Foster, Guyden, and Miller, *Affirmed Action*.

19. Marybeth Gasman, "An Ivy League Professor on Why Colleges Don't Hire More Faculty of Color: 'We Don't Want Them,'" *Washington Post*, September 26, 2016; Caroline Sotello, Viernes Turner, and Samuel L. Myers Jr., *Faculty of Color in Academe: Bittersweet Success* (New York: Allyn and Bacon, 2000).

20. Clifton Conrad and Marybeth Gasman, *Educating a Diverse Nation: Lessons from Minority Serving Institutions* (Cambridge, MA: Harvard University Press, 2015); Aaron Clauset, Samuel Arbesman, and Daniel B. Larre-

more, "Systematic Inequality and Hierarchy in Faculty Hiring Networks," *Science Advances* 1, no. 1 (2015).

21. Solorzano, Ceja, and Yosso, "Critical Race Theory."

22. Jiyun Elizabeth L. Shin, Sheri R. Levy, and Bonita London, "Effect of Role Model Exposure on STEM and non-STEM Student Engagement," *Journal of Applied Social Psychology* 46 (2016): 410–427.

7. A CULTURE OF FAMILY

1. Marybeth Gasman, Dorsey Spencer, and Cecilia Orphan, "'Building Bridges, Not Fences': A History of Civic Engagement at Private Black Colleges and Universities, 1944–1965," *History of Education Quarterly* 55, no. 3 (2015): 346–379.

2. Nicole M. Stephens, Sarah S. M. Townsend, Hazel Rose Markus, and L. Taylor Phillips, "A Cultural Mismatch: Independent Cultural Norms Produce Greater Increases in Cortisol and More Negative Emotions among First-Generation College Students," *Journal of Experimental Social Psychology* 48, no. 6 (2012): 1389–1393.

3. Elaine Seymour and Nancy M. Hewitt, *Talking about Leaving: Why Undergraduates Leave the Sciences* (Boulder, CO: Westview, 1997).

4. Carol B. Stack, *All Our Kin: Strategies for Survival in a Black Community* (New York: Basic Books, 1975); Nicole M. Stephens, MarYam G. Hamedani, Hazel Rose Markus, Hilary B. Bergsieker, and Liyam Eloul, "Why Did They 'Choose' to Stay? Perspectives of Hurricane Katrina Observers and Survivors," *Psychological Science* 20, no. 7 (2009): 878–886.

5. Linda M. Chatters, Robert Joseph Taylor, and Rukmalie Jayakody, "Fictive Kinship Relations in Black Extended Families," *Journal of Comparative Family Studies* (1994): 297–312.

6. Seymour and Hewitt, *Talking about Leaving*.

7. Brown was 75 at the time of the study.

8. National Science Foundation, "Louis Stokes Alliances for Minority Participation (LSAMP)," https://www.nsf.gov/funding/pgm_summ.jsp?pims_id=13646.

9. Heidi B. Carlone and Angela Johnson, "Understanding the Science Experiences of Successful Women of Color: Science Identity as an Analytic Lens," *Journal of Research in Science Teaching* 44, no. 8 (2007): 1187–1218.

10. Errin Haines Whack, "Small University Outranks Many Others in Black Physics Grads," *U.S. News and World Report,* May 26, 2017.

11. Adam Grant, *Give and Take: The Revolutionary Worldview That Drives Success* (New York: Weidenfeld & Nicolson, 2013) and *Give and Take: Why Helping Others Drives Our Success* (Penguin Books: New York, reprint ed., 2014); Mercedes Lorenzo, Catherine H. Crouch, and Eric Mazur, "Reducing the Gender Gap in the Physics Classroom," *American Journal of Physics* 74, no. 2 (2006): 118–122.

8. AN AGENDA FOR THE FUTURE OF STEM

1. Thomas Wood, "Racism Motivated Trump Voters More than Authoritarianism," *Washington Post,* April 17, 2017; Erica Green, "Education Department Says It Will Scale Back Civil Rights Investigations," *New York Times,* June 16, 2017.

2. Patricia M. McDonough, Anthony Lising, Antonio Marybeth Walpole, and Leonor Xochitl Perez, "College Rankings: Democratized College Knowledge for Whom?," *Research in Higher Education* 39, no. 5 (1998): 513–537.

3. Nicole M. Stephens, Stephanie A. Fryberg, Hazel Rose Markus, Camille S. Johnson, and Rebecca Covarrubias, "Unseen Disadvantage: How American Universities' Focus on Independence Undermines the Academic Performance of First-Generation College Students," *Journal of Personality and Social Psychology* 102, no. 6 (2012): 1178.

4. Clifton Conrad, Marybeth Gasman, Todd Lundberg, Thai-Huy Nguyen, Felecia Commodore, and Andrés Castro Samayoa, "Using Educational Data to Increase Learning, Retention, and Degree Attainment at Minority Serving Institutions (MSIs)," Penn Center for Minority Serving Institutions, 2013, https://www.gse.upenn.edu/pdf/cmsi/using_educational _data.pdf; Bi Vuong and Christen Cullum Hairston, "Using Data to Improve Minority-Serving Institution Success," Institute for Higher Education Policy, 2012, http://www.ihep.org/research/publications/using-data -improve-minority-serving-institution-success; Clifton Conrad and Marybeth Gasman, *Educating a Diverse Nation: Lessons from Minority Serving Institutions* (Cambridge, MA: Harvard University Press, 2015).

5. *Washington Monthly* rankings, http://washingtonmonthly.com/college _guide; Marian Thakur, "The Impact of Ranking Systems on Higher Education and Its Stakeholders," *Journal of Institutional Research* 13, no. 1 (2007): 83–96.

6. "STEM," Center on Education and the Workforce, Georgetown University, https://cew.georgetown.edu/cew-reports/stem/#full-report.

CONCLUDING THOUGHTS

1. Aldon Morris, *The Scholar Denied: W. E. B. Du Bois and the Birth of Modern Sociology* (Oakland: University of California Press, 2015).

2. Rob K. Toutkoushian and Michael Paulsen, *Economics of Higher Education* (New York: Springer, 2016).

APPENDIX

1. "Agriculture & Human Sciences," *Prairie View A&M University*, http://www.pvamu.edu/research/active-research/research-centers /agriculture-human-sciences.

2. Deborah Saunders White, North Carolina Central University's chancellor, passed away in 2016.

3. Joshua Berlinger, "Baltimore Riots: A Timeline," *CNN*, April 28, 2015.

4. For more information on South Carolina's "Corridor of Shame," see "Corridor of Shame: The Neglect of South Carolina's Rural Schools," www.corridorofshame.com.

ACKNOWLEDGMENTS

The moment we stepped foot on the campuses of the historically Black colleges or universities (HBCUs) in this study, both of us knew that there was something special and unique about the education provided by these important institutions. There is a sense that greatness has walked, and continues to walk, across the yard. We feel fortunate to have had the opportunity to learn from the ten HBCUs featured in this book and to demonstrate for the larger higher education world that HBCUs possess immense knowledge and creativity that should be recognized and adopted by colleges and universities more generally. Although the HBCU environment cannot be replicated, the strategies and approaches to learning in STEM are essential to our moving African Americans and, quite frankly, all students ahead in STEM across the nation.

We are grateful to the faculty, staff, campus leaders, and students at each of the HBCUs for allowing us to spend time with them, for giving so much to this project, for their work on capacity building in STEM for students on their campuses, and for their innovation and creativity in teaching, mentoring, and providing a family environment for their students.

This project benefited from a national advisory board of STEM experts, including Kelly Mack, Charlie Nelms, Caleph Wilson, Louis W. Sullivan, Valerie Lundy Wagner, and honorary member Freeman Hrabowski. We are grateful to these individuals for their work in STEM and their guidance throughout this project.

We are thankful to our family at the Center for Minority Serving Institutions, who have supported us throughout the research and writing of this book. Many people assisted with gathering data and literature, preliminary coding, and ensuring the accuracy of our claims (Felecia Commodore, Andrés Castro Samayao, William Casey Boland, Melanie Wolff, DeShaun Bennett, Levon Esters, Andrew Martinez, Carol Sandoval, Carmen Ye, Vera Zhang, Briana O'Neal, and Amanda Washington). Others have assisted with the national report (Chris Jimenez) and national convening (Paola Esmieu) that sprang from this project, while still others managed the subcontracts for the capacity-building grants that were given to the ten HBCUs (Carolyn Nalewajko). We are also thankful to others at the Center, including Tope Ligali, William Ndeh Anyu, Jennifer Yang, Marietess Masulit, and Daniel Blake. #centerlove.

This book would not have been possible without the support of the Helmsley Trust's kind donation to our research. In 2014, with the launch of the Center for Minority Serving Institutions, the Trust awarded us $1.5 million to complete this research project. We are particularly thankful to Ryan Kelsey and Sue Cui, our program officers, for believing in this study and seeing HBCUs as what they are—leaders in STEM. Although not funders of this specific project, we would be remiss if we did not thank our core funders at the Center for Minority Serving Institutions, because they support our day-to-day operations. Support from the Kresge Foundation (Caroline Altman Smith, William Moses, Chera Reid, and Rebecca Villarreal) and Educational Testing Service (Michael Nettles and Catherine Millett) is central to the work we do.

Lastly, we would like to thank our family and friends for always supporting us as we travel, write, and research. Marybeth offers special thanks to Thai-Huy Nguyen for being a wonderful co-author; Camille Charles, Yvette Booker, Alice Ginsberg, Michael Nettles, Levon Esters, Sultan Jenkins, Andrés Castro Samayoa, Paola "Lola" Esmieu, and Michael Sorrell for their friendship; Lilly Van Zandt for being an amazing mother and confidant; and Chloe Sarah Epstein for being a reason for living, writing, and breathing daily.

Thai-Huy offers special thanks to Marybeth Gasman for her willingness to take a chance on a rather unconventional candidate for a PhD program. There are no words to express his gratitude for the opportunities and support she has provided to realize his best self. To his mother, Lien Nguyen, he is thankful for the countless sacrifices she has made so that her sons can achieve their own dreams. Thai-Huy also offers thanks to his brothers, Joe and Paul, and his sister-in-law, Jana, for their many expressions of love and care, particularly during times of challenge and transition. He is grateful for the friendship and guidance he has received from Camille Charles, Margo Brooks Carthon, Clifton Conrad, and Michael Nettles. This book was drafted in his second year as a faculty member at Seattle University, where he has had the pleasure of working with wonderful colleagues, Erica Yamamura, Erin Swezey, and Kerry Von Esch. He thanks them for their wisdom, understanding, and overwhelming support. He also could not have successfully balanced multiple studies without his project manager, Rose Ann Gutierrez, and research associates, Nic Lee and Willa Kurland. And to his dear friends, who have been present for moments of both joy and sadness, Thai-Huy sends his gratitude to Christine Gibo Crapps, Adam Hillier, Jacy Crapps, Priscilla

Zee, Larissa Woskob Castner, Kriti Sehgal, Alyssa D'Alconzo Thomas, Dawn Mokuau, David Low, and Mike Nguyen. He also acknowledges and expresses special thanks to Dolly Nguyen, his dear friend and collaborator, for pushing and encouraging him to explore an endless pool of ideas—#NguyenING. To Andrés Castro Samayao, Thai-Huy is thankful for his friendship, encouraging him when others did not, and for challenging him when he needed it the most. And lastly, Thai-Huy recognizes his husband, Leonard Smith, for walking the path of life with him, for his unconditional love, and for supporting him in all his endeavors—for that he is forever grateful.

INDEX

high school. *See* college readiness; education, K-12; preparation; secondary school

Hill, Byron, 41

Hinton, Marge, 132–133

historically black colleges and universities (HBCUs): *Brown v. Board of Education* and, 7; campus visits, 14; culture of collaboration at, 62–91; culture of family at, 143–166; culture of STEM at, 13–14; curriculum at, 12; disregard for achievements of, 7–8; diversity among, 184; faculty at (*see* faculty, at HBCUs); funding for, 6; history of, 5–8; history of success of African Americans at, 16, 94–100, 168, 178; inclusivity at, 92–108; increase in enrollment, 11; integration and, 7–8; learning environment of, 144–145; national exposure for, 185; perception of, 7; relations with Black communities, 143–144; selection of for study, 183–184; statistics about, 20. *See also* higher education; individual colleges and universities

home-life circumstances: acknowledging, 39; college readiness and, 48–49; institutional responsibility

and, 59; racism and, 52. *See also* background, students'; college readiness; preparation

Hrabowski, Freeman, 16

Hunter, Dina, 67

Hurricane Katrina, 161–162

Huston-Tillotson University, 13; culture of family at, 156–159; described, 186, 195–196; non-Black faculty at, 137–138. *See also* historically black colleges and universities (HBCUs)

inclusivity, 92–108, 169–170

independence, 62

individualism, 80, 110, 173. *See also* competition

Inside Higher Education (online news site), 9

institutional responsibility, 34–60; acknowledging / knowing students, 36–40; enacting, 169; expanding notion of college readiness, 43–51; getting to know Black students, 58; guidelines for developing, 57–60; home-life circumstances and, 59; questioning assumptions used to teach / support students, 58–59; reframing narrative, motivation, and skills,

parental involvement, 23

parenting, racial differences in, 23

parents: Black, 23–24; exposure to
higher education, 24

Parker, Terri, 46, 53–54

PASS (Peer Assisted Study Sessions),
50–51, 81–84

passions, identifying / cultivating,
119

PCI (Premedical Concept Institute),
74–80

Peer Assisted Study Sessions (PASS),
50–51, 81–84

peer instructors, 71–73

peers: accountability and, 74–80;
college transition and, 62; culture
of family and, 154; interactions
with, 61–62; Peer Assisted Study
Sessions (PASS), 50–51, 81–84;
perseverance through collaboration and, 84–89; Pre-Freshman
Accelerated Curriculum in
Engineering (PACE), 85–89;
Premedical Concept Institute
(PCI), 74–80; prioritizing community among, 78, 80; stereotypes
and, 62; student instructors, 66–71;
supplemental instruction, 71–73.
See also collaboration

Pell Grants, 21

perseverance, through collaboration, 84–89

Philadelphia Negro, The (Du Bois), 7

physicians. *See* doctors, Black;
medical school

placement exams, 44

Porter, Bill, 102–104

potential: acknowledging, 38–39;
indications of, 65; seeing, 170;
students' perception of, 163–164

poverty, 21. *See also* background,
students'; socioeconomic status

Prairie View A&M University, 13, 74;
acknowledging students' background at, 51; African American
success and, 98–101; culture of
family at, 146–156; culture of
success at, 102–104; described, 186,
189–190; faculty at, 133; Premedical
Concept Institute (PCI), 74–80.
See also historically black colleges
and universities (HBCUs)

pre-college context, 21–25. *See also*
background, students'; college
readiness; education, K-12; home-
life circumstances; preparation

predominantly white institutions
(PWIs), 6; Black students' experi-
ences at, 1–4, 26, 27; culture of
STEM and, 12–13; faculty at, 10–11,

93; funding for, 6; privileging of faculty members' research at, 113; race relations at, 8–9; racial violence at, 9, 11–12; racism and, 92–93; as standard, 16; success of African Americans at, 9, 94; whitewashing of past by, 95. *See also* higher education

Pre-Freshman Accelerated Curriculum in Engineering (PACE), 85–89

Premedical Concept Institute (PCI), 74–80

preparation: overcoming lack of, 172–173; rectifying inequalities in, 65; supplemental instruction, 71–73. *See also* college readiness; education, Black; education, K-12; secondary school

problem-based models, 118

professionalism, preparing students for, 155–156

progress, measuring / sharing, 174

PWIs (predominantly white institutions). *See* predominantly white institutions (PWIs)

race: in American education, 37; current environment and, 167; recognizing student needs and, 36; support of students and, 35–36

race relations, at PWIs, 8–9

racial inequality, addressing, 178

racial violence, 9, 11–12

racism: effects of, 52, 92–93; in higher education, 5, 6, 11, 17; institutional responsibility and, 52; at PWIs, 92–93. *See also* stereotypes

reading skills, 23

Reid, Greg, 37, 38, 48–49, 52, 53, 56–57

research, 82–83, 109–110, 121–123, 175

Riegle, Catherine, 30

Roberts, Daryl, 48, 55, 120

role models, same-gender, same-race, 130, 132–142. *See also* peers

same-gender, same-race faculty / role models, 130, 132–142

school districts, segregation in, 22

science: competition in, 33; racism in, 10; women in, 159–164. *See also* science, technology, engineering, and mathematics (STEM)

science, technology, engineering, and mathematics (STEM). *See* engineering; mathematics; science; STEM (science, technology, engineering, and mathematics); STEM, culture of

science courses: high school, 30, 31;
introductory, 32; preparation for,
41. *See also* gateway courses
secondary school: college eligibility /
readiness and, 25; college preparatory courses, 29; unequal access
to / enrollment in STEM classes
in, 31. *See also* background, students'; college readiness; education,
Black; education, K-12; preparation
segregation, 7, 22
self-direction, 62
self-doubt, 52–57
self-motivation, 56
Seymour, Elaine, 33
Shaw, Lynette, 98, 145, 146–151
similar-race working groups,
79–80
slavery, 17
social justice, 175–176
social mobility, 176
social realities, 39. *See also* background, students'; home-life
circumstances
socioeconomic status, 21, 35–36
sociology, 7
South Carolina, education in,
39–40
staff, 34. *See also* institutional
responsibility

Stanford University, 32
Steele, Claude, 27–28
STEM (science, technology,
engineering, and mathematics):
agenda for diversity in, 169–177;
minority departure from, 31; need
for diversity in, 168; positive results
for African Americans in, 16, 168;
underrepresentation of African
Americans in, 4–5, 20, 84; women
in, 159–164. *See also* engineering;
gateway courses; mathematics;
science
STEM, culture of, 55; changing, 15;
competition in, 62–63; dominance
by White men, 81; at HBCUs,
13–14; individualism in, 80; insights
into, 160–161; at PWIs, 12–13; racist /
exclusionary nature of, 12–13,
16–17; stereotype threat and, 28
STEM education: daily exposure to
curricula, 172–173; data-driven
intervention pertaining to,
184–185; HBCUs' success in, 178;
high school, 30–31; linking to
social justice, 175–176; minority
achievement in, 176; rethinking,
168
stereotypes, 25–28; faculty assumptions about students and, 37;

success (*continued*)
   See also achievement; doctors,
   Black; medical school
Sullivan, Louis W., 94
summer boot camp, 119
supplemental instruction, 71–73
support of students, 35; by faculty,
   110–128; proactive, 172; for White
   students, 89–90; at Xavier University, 64–71. *See also* collaboration;
   home-life circumstances; institutional responsibility; peers
syllabus, 112. *See also* curricula

Taylor, Linda, 112–113, 115
teachers. *See* faculty
teaching: across curriculum, 114;
   questioning modes of, 168;
   rewarding, 174–175
teaching assistants, 124, 171
teaching styles, 59
teamwork: by faculty, 112–123.
   See also collaboration; peers
tenure system, 110, 175
tests. *See* exams
textbooks, reading, 118
time management skills, 76
Tisdale, Henry, 34, 35
TMI (too much information), 157
Toma, Akil, 136, 145, 159–164

too much information (TMI), 157
transition to college. *See* college
   transition
Treisman, Uri, 16, 80
Trump, Donald, 9
trust, 146
Turner, Eric, 42, 43
tutors, student, 66–73

United Negro College Fund, 17
universities. *See* higher education;
   historically black colleges and
   universities (HBCUs)
urban regions, 21

videos, faculty, 126
violence, racial, 9, 11–12
Virginia, University of, 26
visibility, of Black students, 37–38

Ware, Sally, 113, 116–117, 119, 125
Waters, Rachel, 145, 156–159
White flight, 21–22
White privilege, 137
Wiley, Alice, 126
Wilkins, Barry, 37, 117–118
Williams, Denise, 54–55
women: exclusionary nature of
   STEM and, 62; microaggressions
   and, 131; in science, 159–164

women, Black, 81; biases against in STEM, 137; on faculty (*see* faculty, Black women); in STEM, 159–164

Woods, Bernice, 76

Xavier University of Louisiana, 8, 13; Black doctors from, 138; Black women faculty at, 133, 135; Chemistry Resource Center, 69–71; collaboration at, 69–71; coordination / connectedness among faculty at, 112–117, 124–125; culture of success at, 104–108; described, 186, 187–188; drill system at, 65–69, 112, 115–117; exams at, 117; faculty at, 119; learning through collaboration at, 63–71; success of African Americans and, 95–98; support of students at, 64–71. *See also* historically black colleges and universities (HBCUs)

Yun, John, 25